HISTORIC HOTELS
of
COLUMBUS
OHIO

HISTORIC HOTELS
of
COLUMBUS OHIO

TOM BETTI & DOREEN UHAS SAUER

For Columbus Landmarks Foundation

THE
History
PRESS

Published by The History Press
Charleston, SC 29403
www.historypress.net

First published 2015

Manufactured in the United States

ISBN 978.1.62619.896.8

Library of Congress Control Number: 2015943856

This book is dedicated to the memory of our dear friend (and Hartman Building neighbor) Anne Marshall Saunier, who inspired many, taught us much, listened intensely, had such a passion for life, gave us the truth and laughed at our jokes whether they were funny or not. We miss you, Anne.

CONTENTS

PREFACE

When we decided to write about Columbus's historic hotels, we assumed that the grande dames of a bygone era—the Deshler, the Neil House, the Chittenden, the Hartman and the Great Southern—would make up five tidy chapters. From our writing and researching of Columbus's historic taverns, we assumed that there would be some surprises. We did not expect to find more than two hundred drinking establishments in Columbus in the 1890s. And so it was with hotels.

The more we researched hotels, the harder it became to limit ourselves to just five establishments. When we asked people what downtown hotels they remembered (whether or not the building still existed), a number of hotels surfaced in their memories—the Seneca, the Norwich, Fort Hayes, the Northern, the Park and the Metropole. Others were names from their parents' memories—the Charminel, the Farmers, the Columbus, the Macon, the St. Clair and the Star.

Forget the hotel chains that came to Columbus in the 1970s through the 1990s, like the Sheraton and the Hyatt, and don't even go there with the chain motels like Holiday Inn, Howard Johnson or the mom-and-pop roadside architectural wonders like Forty Winks, the Bambi or the Homestead—we had enough on our hands.

Tom and I both grew up in Cleveland, a city rich in historic hotels, which may account for our fascination with them. Though more than a generation apart in age, by working together on the board of trustees at the Columbus Landmarks Foundation, Tom and I discovered we shared an affinity for the stories behind buildings, a love of local history and Cleveland's immigrant DNA.

While Tom now lives in a condo in one of Columbus's most elegant former hotels, the Hartman, my connection to Columbus hotels is different. I arrived in Columbus thirty years before Tom, and I was fortunate to have seen with my own eyes the Neil House and the Deshler. As a college student boldly curious about making a new city my home, I checked out the lobbies, restaurants, restrooms and especially the watering holes of Columbus—places for people watching.

Tom's fascination with hotels has led him to haunt the finest establishments in Cincinnati; London; New York City; Chicago; Washington, D.C.; and West Baden, Indiana. At these places, it is easy to remember how history has played out for the rich, the famous, the powerful and the pretenders.

My own brush with hotels was more the personal; I worked at the Ohio Stater Inn across from Ohio State University (OSU). Legendary coach Woody Hayes and comedian Jonathan Winters were more than occasional solitary diners on my shift in the middle of the afternoon. Columbus mayor Maynard Sensenbrenner (1954–59, 1964–71) had monthly city meetings and appearances at banquets where he handed out American flag pins and kept, in his words, a watch on the university to "keep those damned kids under control." (It was the era of jaywalking protests and, later, antiwar demonstrations.) I found out things about hotels I didn't want to know, and I was fascinated by the backstories of those who worked in them and those who frequented them.

A well-known early Columbus TV personality and an honored Catholic Father of the Year had a weekly scheduled "nooner" at the inn after lunching with his girlfriend. The bartender, Annie, was a voluptuous red-headed Elizabeth Taylor look-alike who had had hard luck stories of her own but mothered all the college waitresses, most of the English Department (drunk or sober) and the many traveling salesmen who could not afford the downtown hotels.

As with any workplace, the people who ran the show behind the scenes had the most compelling stories. The cooks and dishwashers were from Alabama families who arrived with the Great Migration and who now led civil rights pickets at the downtown dime stores on their days off. The three-time married manager who spent his eighteenth birthday in a cockpit bombing North Korea still suffered from post-traumatic stress disorder, often while on the job. The hotel manager and part-time "hotel dick" (detective), the son of a once-prominent Haitian family, came for OSU business courses but could afford to learn business only by working full time.

This is what Tom and I both learned, each in our own way, while researching the book: in reality, hotels are made of a series of rooms where hopes, vendettas, power plays and secrets run like a continuous loop on a projector—much like history itself. Hotels have lives—they are conceived, born, age, often partner with other hotels, sometimes pass on, become the actual "dust" in the ashbin of history or are reborn. There were over 125 hotels in downtown Columbus in the one-hundred-year-span from the mid-nineteenth century to the mid-twentieth century. These are only a fraction of their stories.

As with our previous books, Tom and I would like to acknowledge members of the Education Committee of Columbus Landmarks Foundation for all their help and the Columbus Landmarks Foundation board for continuing to support our notion that a brick is just a brick unless there is a story behind it. Special thanks to Ann Seren and Terry Sherburn for passing along stories and research and to the staff of the Local History and Genealogical Society Division of the Columbus Metropolitan Library; they are wonderful, generous, humorous and very knowledgeable people.

DOREEN UHAS SAUER

INTRODUCTION

One morning, in the fall of 1880, a middle-aged woman, accompanied by a young girl of eighteen, presented herself at the clerk's desk of the principal hotel in Columbus, Ohio, and made inquiry about whether there was anything about the place she could do. She was of a helpless, fleshy build, with a frank, open countenance and an innocent, diffident manner…Anyone could see where the daughter behind her got the timidity and shamefacedness, which now caused her to stand back and look indifferently away.

And so, Theodore Dreiser, an American realist writer (1871–1945), opened his novel *Jennie Gerhardt* (1911). Jennie is an innocent, impoverished young girl in Columbus who will be seduced by George Brander, a United States senator, at the Neil House.

In 1911, sex before marriage—much less between people of two different social and economic classes—would be told as a cautionary tale, not to be moralistic but to be realistic. No happy ending here. The daughter of German immigrants, Jennie is seduced in the hotel; becomes an unwed mother; goes on to other men, other promises and another love (he marries someone else); loses her daughter; and becomes a silent and secret mourner at her lover's funeral.

What does this have to do with Columbus hotels? Why does Dreiser's tale begin in a Columbus hotel? And it's not just any hotel, but the grand Neil House across from the Ohio Statehouse.

The Neil House Hotel and the Deshler Hotel were landmarks in the downtown skyline for many years. Both were gone by 1981. *Columbus Metropolitan Library Image Collection.*

Indiana-born Dreiser probably passed through Columbus a dozen times. He knew people and their temptations. In 1911, Columbus was a railroad town, a town that was growing rich, and Dreiser routinely traveled from Chicago to Pittsburgh, St. Louis and New York, which would have brought him through Columbus. He was a writer and reporter who rubbed elbows with those of the many classes who traveled the rails. The transportation and socioeconomic changes happening in America played out in that most public (and yet most private space)—the hotel, a byproduct of the stage coach, the wagon and especially the railroad. From the end of the Civil War to the beginning of the Depression, railroads grew.

In 1929, over 150 passenger trains a day still came through Columbus, but few realized twenty thousand cars and trucks were already on the eleven highways in Columbus, and a new transcontinental air service in the city was just starting at the same time. Hotels were doomed even as they glittered.

Yet for the nineteenth and most of the early twentieth centuries, party politics thrived in the post–Civil War era of Northern prosperity. The Statehouse was the hub of power, and this created a special need for hotels. The Neil House on High Street had been there since the 1830s. It is said more deals happened in the Neil House bar than on the legislative floor.

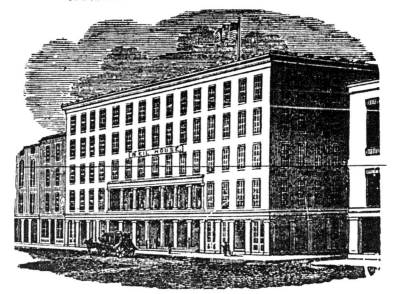

NEIL HOUSE,

OPPOSITE THE MAIN ENTRANCE TO THE CAPITOL.

WALSTEIN FAILING, - - - - - - - - - PROPRIETOR.

An early newspaper advertisement in the 1840s of the first Neil House Hotel, located across from the Ohio Statehouse. *Columbus Metropolitan Library Image Collection.*

The need for taverns with sleeping areas (or the use of the barroom floor), boardinghouses and/or hotels predates the Neil House by three decades. Travelers and their horses faced only wilderness without a tavern or hotel. Wheeled mail and passenger service began (1816) with Phillip Zinn's coaches between Columbus and Chillicothe, increasing the need for hotels even more.

Tavern and hotel keeping were early occupations. The Lion and the Eagle (later called the Globe), the Columbus Inn (later called the City House), the Red Lion Hotel, the White Horse Tavern (later called the Eagle Hotel) and Swan's Tavern, which included a bakery (later known as the Franklin House), were some of the early establishments. Names changed frequently in early Columbus—the Swan was later the Sheaf of Wheat; McCullom's Tavern was also the Black Bear.

With the appearance of the first canalboat in Columbus (1831), the population and wealth of the city grew. From 1,500 people in Columbus in

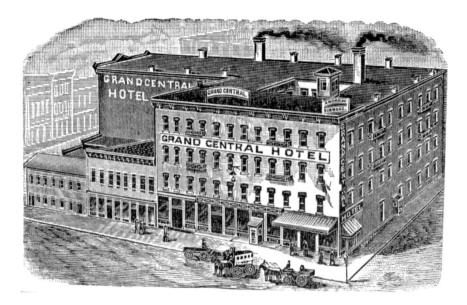

The Grand Central Hotel was one of Columbus's many nineteenth-century hotels that served guests who arrived by railroad. It advertised "first class accommodations: $2.00 to $2.50 a night, Andrew Schwarz, proprietor." It operated from 1890 to 1898. *Columbus Metropolitan Library Image Collection.*

1827, there were 25,000 thirty years later. The number of hotels increased even more with the arrival of the railroads.

Railroad service began in Columbus in 1850, when the first train to run on the Columbus and Xenia Railroad departed from Xenia. Because of the National Road and the feeder canal, Columbus became a crossroads city—a place to pass through for the gold fields of California or the farms of Nebraska. Yet some stayed—immigrants, entrepreneurs and investors. With the railroads and the prominence of Ohio in national politics, hotels flourished—grand ones for emerging politicians, industrialists, self-made men used to making deals and men who sometimes preyed on the help.

Grand hotels depended on the low-paying jobs they provided. Myriad porters, cleaning ladies, barbers, cooks, maids, waiters, bartenders, flower girls, housekeepers, furnace tenders, carpenters, bellhops and dishwashers lived on low salaries and tips. These jobs were filled mostly by African Americans and, later, by female immigrants, but both were the most vulnerable population in the frequent recessions and depressions of the times.

At the same time, there were respectable, good hotels and boardinghouses. There were also seedy hotels. Some establishments catered to a specific clientele—passengers who needed only a one night stay, temperance-minded travelers who did not want to be in a hotel where others might drink, young men who lived in housekeeping arrangements to accommodate their bachelor status and salesmen.

Columbus was the founding city for the United Commercial Travelers Union (UCTU), a fraternal group that provided insurance for traveling salesmen and their families. Dreiser, who started his writing career as a reporter, frequently traveled to cover stories from meatpacking to modern art and to interview the literary and industrial celebrities of his day. Characters in his novel, especially salesmen, are frequently judged by their choice of clothes and accommodations. Traveling salesmen had acquired a dubious reputation and were, according to the UCTU, an under-appreciated lot who were also known by a strange nickname: "knights of the grip."

From the post–Civil War era to World War I, Columbus was a huge convention city because of the railroads. Columbus was situated within a five-hundred-mile radius that could be reached by seventy-five million people. The board of trade (later renamed the more modern term "chamber of commerce") pumped out advertising for the city to reach the millions in this area.

Hotels—a second home to salesmen, businessmen and reporters—also beckoned scammers and charlatans (Columbus was known as a "city of rubes" who easily accepted a get-rich scheme). And then there were the not-so-proper ladies. Good hotels were moral hotels that suffered no fools and no shenanigans. Sinners beware.

In July 1868, over a period of a few days, the *Ohio State Journal* reported on a seduction case at the Galt House (178 North High Street), following the shocking story to its surprising conclusion. On a Monday morning, what started as a story in a rival newspaper was reexamined by the reporters of the *Ohio State Journal*. A sixteen-year-old girl, Emma Jordan, was violated by a pilot of the steamship *Charmer*.

While one can conclude that Mr. Devine, the pilot of the steamship, was certainly not piloting on the canal, no reason is given for why he was coming from Indianapolis, and no reporter pointed out that the names "*Charmer*" and "Devine" seemed a bit ironic. The Galt House was happy to assist in an investigation, proving to the public its role had been to root out moral turpitude.

The clerk at the hotel had his own reasons for believing a clandestine meeting had been prearranged between the girl and Devine. The porter of the hotel was posted at an angle in the hall to make observations. Immediately after the gentleman retired, the girl was seen entering his room. Word was given to the clerk, who went and demanded admittance into the room.

Devine refused. The clerk, the porter and the hotel proprietor attempted to break down the door. When Devine relented, there was no young girl. Devine cursed them for thinking evil. The girl's room was also empty. But someone was seen walking over the skylight during all the excitement. There were other hotel room windows along the skylight, and Jordan was ultimately found under the bed of an old gentleman from Kentucky.

In the confusion, Jordan had leapt from Devine's window to the skylight, entered the room of the old man and begged him "in piteous tones to protect her." She gained his sympathy, and he refused to admit the porter until the hotel staff threatened to force the door open. Devine was arrested. Jordan escaped the hotel and was found on Pearl Street. She had been part of a group traveling from Pittsburgh to St. Louis with a "preacher" who had "ruined" her, procuring his damaged goods for Devine at the depot.

The old man from Kentucky "firmly declared his intention to keep out of the city during the few remaining years of his life." Theodore Dreiser could have written the story.

Cover-ups were probably frequent. Even a cursory look at nineteenth-century Columbus crime reveals a multitude of sex-related crimes—brothels pretending to be decent boardinghouses; street walkers; trafficked children; fornications and adulterous rendezvous; botched abortions; pimping, pandering and seduction in hotels; and even an occasional unnatural affection for an animal.

However, the ideal of hotels for women only (to protect them) also had its drawbacks. The *Daily Dispatch* (forerunner of the *Columbus Evening Dispatch*) went to considerable length in 1878 to warn of such an idea that backfired in New York. A hotel for women only closed after just two months but planned to reopen soon as a hotel for both sexes. A New York judge said, "The Woman's Hotel is a failure…as manager of the estate it [is] upon me to save the estate from being burdened from any additional expense by turning the hotel to some profitable use." Over $3 million had been invested in this reasonably priced hotel. It was beautiful, safe and comfortable with a uniquely decorated, vast library; $300,000 in art; exceptional food; and imported porcelain—all designed for the working girl. But the women's hotel could not get even fifty boarders to stay from the two hundred accepted applicants. Why?

"They promised and promised and promised to come, but admitted that they would rather stay where the men were," reported the newspaper. In the end, only fifteen women—all homeless—wanted to stay. The women, it was said, would rather stay at boardinghouses and put up with hall bedrooms or poor food than sacrifice men. Others were afraid gossip would lead to scandal, and the term "working girls" would mean something much different.

The hotel had to go co-ed; its transformation would include smoking rooms, a barbershop, a billiard room and a saloon.

Hotels were expected to be welcoming, though not in Jordan's case. In 1864, during the tension of the Civil War, a scandal was exposed by the *Ohio State Journal* (a newspaper that prided itself on being called "the old ventilator" because it exposed the city's dirty laundry). A legless veteran had fallen down stairs and was "taken for dead." His comrades carried him to a nearby hotel, but they were refused admittance by the proprietor, who was a Copperhead (meaning either a Southern sympathizer or a Democrat). They offered money. He refused, saying, "It was not expected that he take in soldiers and care for them." Another veteran remarked he knew the proprietor's son was a quartermaster at Camp Chase, though the father was pro-South. The newspaper pronounced a harsh verdict on the hotel owner: "A man who would refuse to extend aid to such a man is unfit to do business for the public—is too mean to live, and ought to hang himself at the first opportunity."

Papers often reported on the more unexpected hotel guests. A news item in 1824 noted that Major Taliaserro, the agent for Indian affairs at St. Peter's, stayed at Tennison's Hotel in Franklinton with delegations of Sioux, Chippewa and Menomonies, tribes from the upper Mississippi, that were on their way to visit government officials in Washington, D.C.

Another news item from 1853 exclaimed the greatest wonder of the age could be seen at "Neil's new Hall." Major Ver Hines of Tennessee would give one of his amusing entertainments. The entertainment? Staring at the major, who was only thirty inches tall and weighted thirty pounds. He was twenty four years old, "well proportioned, and...good-looking." According to the ladies, he was the successful rival to Tom Thumb, who, by the way, was also stared at in the Neil House.

1

SO MANY TO CHOOSE FROM

NINETEENTH-CENTURY COLUMBUS TAVERNS, BOARDINGHOUSES AND HOTELS

W as that Mrs. McMurdy's or Mrs. McCullogh's boardinghouse?" a confused traveler to Columbus might ask.

Not to be confusing, but Mrs. McCullough ran a boardinghouse on the southeast corner of Town and Front Streets at the same time Mrs. McMurdy ran her boardinghouse between State and Broad Streets. And herein lies a problem in early Columbus: with no Expedia or Google, remembering what accommodation was where was more than a little confusing. Of course, no one probably called ahead for reservations, and travelers were wise to check the local newspapers for ads that published specific locations and/or name changes of hotels.

There was no shortage of rooms. Travelers who needed overnight accommodations in nineteenth-century Columbus had plenty to choose from. The number of hotels and boardinghouses listed in city directories and local newspaper is astonishing. Though mostly centered by the old Union Depot (today the site of the convention center), some hotels were clustered around Capitol Square and legislative offices. Others were in scattered nodes across the city.

The Buckeye Hotel was on East Broad Street immediately across from the Statehouse (the present-day site of the James Rhodes Office Tower) and was popular with the legislators, as were the National Hotel and the American Hotel.

A number of hotels were located on Third Street or Gay Street. More were around the river where the canal came into Columbus. The Mansion

Early frame hotels that were sometimes expanded boardinghouses, such as the Hotel Boyer, were the first to be replaced by more substantial buildings. *Columbus Metropolitan Library Image Collection.*

House (or Mansion Hotel) was here, signaling the need for accommodations near this gateway to the city. Canalboats traveled up and down the Scioto River, and smaller hotels and boardinghouses were clustered in this area (approximately where Bicentennial Park is today). McCune's Canal Boat Dock was on the west side of Friend Street (now Main Street), and J. Zettler had a boardinghouse near Rich and Friend Streets. (More on the Zettler establishment later.)

The Scioto Hotel advertised itself as being near the canal bridge; then later on the west side of the head of the canal; then on the north side of Main, west of the canal; then on the south side, west of the canal (65 West Main Street); then the northwest corner of Main and Canal (now approximately where Civic Center Drive is); and then at 148 West Main Street. Either the hotel changed locations frequently or pinpointing an exact address near the boat docks was impossible. The Scioto Hotel appears to have lasted from the 1840s to the 1870s.

Older establishments on the west side of the river in Franklinton were additional options—like the Walters Hotel (no address given); the Old Cadwallader House; the West Broad Street House, which added thirty-five new bedrooms and had a large stable with twenty-five stalls and a shed to hold wagons and carriages. The West Broad Street House (no address given) marketed to a traveler different from the Union Depot crowd; it was the best location for farmers and manufacturers (obviously coming by means of their own transportation).

In between the hotels were boardinghouses—popular options for travelers and long-term stays for legislators. They were often run by women, like Mrs. Ware's Boarding House (Third Street between Main and Rich Streets) and Mrs. Ann Scott's Boarding House (Third Street near State Street). Both operated in the 1840s. The emphasis on the prefix "Mrs." lent an air of respectability that might otherwise be lost on an establishment with rooms to let and run by a woman. Some boardinghouses eventually turned into hotels—after a man purchased the boardinghouse site.

However, in one case, a great emphasis was placed on the fact that the hotel was owned by a woman, Mrs. N.J. Lattimer Williams. Described in the 1878 *Industries of Ohio*, Williams was said to have the tact that is positively essential to the successful management of a hotel. "Though a woman," she knew more about running a hotel than "eight tenths of the men engaged in the difficult business." The Williams Hotel (120 North High Street) appealed to the hungry. Williams's table was "at all times supplied to repletion with all the delicacies and substantials [*sic*] of the season, and cooked in that style that is so acceptable to the epicure." It did not hurt that she had a resident storyteller. She was the daughter of an early Columbus "pioneer," Peter Lattimer, who had come to the city when it was still dense wilderness, had only three log huts and wolves roamed "in all their freedom over the ground where the State House stands."

At ninety-seven, Peter Lattimer was a wonderful tale spinner—fully remembering casting his vote for Thomas Jefferson for president and recalling when the town was laid out. If having a bountiful table and a charming, storytelling old father were not enough, Williams had (in 1878) "the only house in the city provided with an elevator."

In addition to hotels and boardinghouses, taverns with accommodations also served Columbus in the first two decades of its founding. The names were colorful and changed frequently. Some had a certain honesty about them. In 1822, Jarvis Pike advertised that his prices "compare with the present depressed state of the times, and the cheapness of living."

The Columbus Inn was the first building that appeared on the southeast corner of Town and High Streets; it was built by David Broderick, who started providing overnight accommodations there in 1815. In later years, a new manager painted a signboard with a rose tree on it, in reference to the adage "the wilderness shall blossom as the rose."

A number of early hotels reflected national pride and were called the Eagle. One hotel in Franklinton took the name "Spread Eagle Hotel," which seems, to today's ear, rather odd. Others named their hotels to make it clear what kind of customers they wanted, like the Temperance House in Franklinton.

Since men and political caucuses generally dominated the taverns and hotels, it was natural that they were associated with the consumption of alcohol. However, there were other options. The Washington Temperance House was started in 1845 by Mr. Alston. Ironically, it was also advertised as a tavern stand (a common term for tavern with accommodations). When it was for sale in 1846, it was advertised as being in good repair with a convenient dining room, a kitchen and a stable that could accommodate thirty horses "with convenient terms"…and only $400 down with the balance in yearly payments.

In 1846, William Tolliver opened a temperance restaurant. In the 1870s, the Temperance Union Home (Spring and North High Streets), "two squares from the Depot," opened. While most hotels advertised the experience and genteel nature of the proprietor as a selling point to potential customers, the Temperance Union Home advertised that Mrs. A.M. Chalfant, the proprietress, was recently the matron of the Ohio Penitentiary. It was "well known in Southern Ohio she possessed unusual business capacity." Temperance people were advised to patronize this well-managed house that cost only one dollar a day.

The Union Stock Yard Hotel was also known over the years as the Central Stock Yard Hotel and the Columbus Stock Yard Hotel and located near Neil (now Neilston) and Mt. Vernon Avenues, where holding pens were situated. In 1841, a Farmers and Mechanics Tavern was advertised as being "near the Bridge" and owned by Thomas Cawallader, a name that appears as owner or manager of other hotels on the west side.

Other options included the Occidental Hotel (126 North Third Street); the O'Harra Boarding House (northwest corner of Gay and North High Streets); the Northwood Resort (no address); the Barr House (334–36 South High); and the Rail Road Exchange (opposite the Union Depot), where breakfast was served "in time for the cars," meals were served at all hours and baggage was conveyed free of charge to and from the trains.

The majority of hotels and boardinghouses were found north of the Statehouse and near the Union Depot. The Union Hotel provided good accommodations for travelers and good stabling for horses on North High Street near Spring and Chestnut Streets. In 1878, the St. James Hotel, formerly known as the Long Street House, was conveniently located on West Long Street, almost at the corner of North High Street. With fifty comfortably furnished rooms, the hotel's reputation was made on an efficient manager who kept his table well supplied and his premises neat and orderly. His motto was "Terms reasonable."

Advertisements and newspaper notices reflect ever-changing ownership and management arrangements. The Barr House was taken over in 1830 by James Robinson, and it also became known as Robinson's Tavern, then the White House and then Robinson's City House (run by Mrs. Robinson and her son). James Robinson and his son also managed the Franklin House at South High and State Streets. In 1824, James Robinson also had owned the Bell Tavern, which became the Red Lion.

On the north side, the Rail Road Exchange later became the Exchange Hotel and then the Powell House. In the 1870s, the Exchange Hotel (also known as Kauffman's Exchange) was in a most advantageous position—almost directly across from the Union Depot. In fact, it was generally referred to as the nearest first-class hotel to Union Station—a place where one could arrive late in the day, stay overnight and not miss an early train in the morning. As was common, "first-class" generally was based on attentive service and reasonable delicacies. The hotel's location also placed it at the hub of action—"chariots" and streetcars passed the doors of the hotel every five minutes, allowing the hotel guest to view any part of the city at a moment's notice.

Geography was a selling point, but when the Exchange became the Powell House twenty years later, the building's landmark placement also put it in harm's way—the carriages, buggies and streetcars (not to mention pedestrian traffic) on North High Street and the many railroad tracks going in and out of the depot crossed one another at the same grade. Something had to give.

The case of *Columbus, Springfield & Cincinnati Railroad v. the City of Columbus* (1871) was over the right of the railroad to buy another portion of the old North Graveyard on the city's northern boundary (North High and Park Streets). The North Graveyard was already decimated by railroads, and residents seem to have suddenly noticed that the dead were contaminating the water supply. The case ruled in favor of the railroads, which were told to compensate the city with the sum of $14,625 for one hundred feet of property.

Within twenty years, the hotel's 1892 passing had been noted in the *Ohio State Journal* with both sadness and acceptance of urban improvements. The hotel was torn down to make way for the new viaduct intended to separate the street traffic from the railroad lines. The building was less than fifty years old, but because of its location, it was widely known. William Powell had originally purchased the land in 1847 for the sole purpose of erecting a hotel. At the time, it was outside the city limits. But this is not a simple tale of the demise of one building; this pattern doomed other hotels.

John Wahlenmeir was the proprietor/owner of an establishment near Main and Rich Streets, also called the Eagle Hotel. His other hotel, the Deutschland Hotel (7–9 Maple Street), was near the depot and in the way of the expansion of the Little Miami railroad tracks in 1874. It was lost. When the third Union Station was built, a bridge was installed over the railroad tracks on North High Street, and other buildings were moved.

The Wahlenmeir European Hotel (northwest corner of North High and Naghten Streets) was managed by John's son, George Wahlenmeir, until 1871. The word "European" was especially prominent for the sake of the many Germans who were arriving through the nearby depot. The hotel itself had a resemblance to hotels in Bavaria, complete with flower boxes. German was spoken at the hotel, and meals were thirty cents. Mrs. Wahlenmeir had cooked her way to America and, on arrival, did not stop, doing much of the hotel's meal preparation. According to a granddaughter, her grandmother even kept a cow or two at the old North Graveyard (where the North Market stands today) to have fresh milk on hand. The family also owned several restaurants and saloons in the area that were relocated, and they also built the Hotel Germania (22 West Naghten Streer) just after the Civil War. In 1956, a picture of the Hotel Germania, later renamed the Deutsches Gasthaus, was given by attorney Francis Thompson to Arthur Avey, a spokesman for the Jehovah's Witnesses, who had acquired the site of the long-razed hotel and the hall that stood in its place.

Progress brought competition for new technology. The National Hotel (not to be confused with the National Hotel across from the Ohio Statehouse) was listed at 272 North High Street and, the following year the name changed to the Davidson European Hotel. The new proprietor advertised modern improvements and elegantly furnished and well-ventilated rooms, with wine and lunch available. Furthermore, his newly renovated hotel was "introducing" water pipes throughout the building, along with Brussels carpets, new paper, new bedsteads and mattresses and marble-top stands. Forget the free Wi-Fi, mother, they have plumbing.

The Ohio Hotel's Sign of the Wheat Sheaf (Friend and South High Streets) advertised in 1821 that it was prepared to "accommodate travelling ladies and gentlemen in decent style" and could house members of the legislature at reasonable prices. It is not clear whether the hotel's offerings were "decent" or if the ladies and gentlemen were expected to be of a "decent" class. In addition to several Ohio Hotels, there were a number of Columbus Inns.

The Pennsylvania House (178 North High Street) operated after the Civil War, not to be confused with the Pittsburgh House only a few doors north. There was also a St. Louis Hotel near the Union Depot at North High and Naghten Streets, formerly called the Wahlenmaier European Hotel. Not to make these names more convoluted, but there was also a Maryland Hotel (formerly the Eagle Hotel; yes, another Eagle) between Town and Rich Streets.

Such specific geographic names often reflected a special arrangement with a railroad that connected Columbus to that location. In the case of the Maryland Hotel, the advertisement that extolled the virtues of the establishment was carried three times weekly in the *Baltimore American* newspaper. Presumably, a recognizable name for Marylanders was a reassuring factor in their choosing a Columbus hotel.

Legislators often boarded at the respectable and more moderately priced taverns, like Russell's Tavern at the corner of South High and Rich Streets. Boarding in the 1830s cost about five dollars a week. Russell must have been one of the most ambitious proprietors; city directories have him listed in a number of locations up and down North and South High Streets. He had a tavern with accommodations as early as 1812, purchased another location in 1818, managed the Globe and the Russell Hotels until 1847 and supervised the United States Hotel until 1850.

Hotel Nelson (northeast corner of Fourth and Friend—now Main—Streets), the Royal House (261½ North High Street) and the Mansion House (near the canal) were well-known hotels in the nineteenth century. Note that "Royal" House perhaps reflected the owner's name and not its rich accommodations; its address indicates that it was at the back of another building.

The Zettler House, different than the previously mentioned boardinghouse, appeared in 1862 on the northeast corner of Friend and Fourth Streets, managed by Jacob Parr of Fairfield County and financed by the Zettler brothers. While most present-day Columbus residents are familiar with the Zettler stores across Columbus, downtowners especially associate the name with Zettler Hardware (101 East Main Street). Zettler House was nearby and considered an authentic (some say "romantic") hotel with a European atmosphere and a distinctive, extensive architectural overhang to shelter carriages.

The Zettlers were nothing if not entrepreneurial; the hotel was formerly on the site where Louis and Jacob Zettler sold produce, liquor and groceries. Louis had arrived in Columbus in 1844 at the age of twelve. He and his brother Jacob made their money from the commerce of the canal—pork and grain. Louis's five sons also bought and sold goods—china, hardware and groceries. In addition to operating hotels, Albert, Frederick and Louis Zettlers sold hardware at 175 East Main Street; Jacob and Edmund sold groceries, lime, plaster and cement at 270 East Main Street; George Zettler worked as a carpenter near Rich and South High Streets; and John Zettler owned a grocery and saloon at Third and Gay Streets—all convenient things to have access to for a hotel.

While the Zettler occupations were rooted in the early canal days, their choice of Main Street for the hotel and grocery business was also a result of the National Road, which entered Columbus from the east. The National Road (historic Route 40) brought a substantial increase in goods, money, immigrants and travelers to Columbus. The National Road House (Main and Fifth Streets) operated from 1843 to 1852. Menely's Tavern and the Columbus House were also convenient for travelers on the National Road.

Other hotels south of the Ohio Statehouse included the Nagle House (South High Street between Rich and Main Streets), the Merchant's Hotel (240 South High Street), the Upton House (South High and Town Streets) and the Montgomery House (South High and Fulton Streets) near the courthouse. Later, the Montgomery House became the Franklin House.

As was typical in hotel advertisements in the 1840s, the new Franklin House praised the "superior accommodations" of the newly purchased hotel but then quickly added that the new owner had repaired all the deficiencies of the previous establishment for "the comfort and convenience of his friends and others who may favor him with their custom."

What were the wants of the traveling public? From the advertisements, it appears that while it was amusing to have a black bear turning a water wheel that provided showers (see *Historic Columbus Taverns*, Tom Betti and Doreen Uhas Sauer) and the availability of food (not necessarily alcohol, since everyone served liquor) was noted, what really mattered was parking. Yes, parking for one's horse. Hotels most often noted their first-rate stables for horses. Those who came with wagons or drays knew there was more parking on the west side of the river (like today).

The Union Hotel was established in 1836 (South High Street near Rich Street and opposite the tavern of Christian Heyl) was not the only establishment to use the name "Union," clearly a patriotic reference that

The Hotel Lincoln was later known as the Broad-Lincoln Hotel and lasted until the mid-twentieth century. *Columbus Metropolitan Library Image Collection.*

predated the Civil War. It advertised as being "at the sign of the Golden Plough." The owner, John Rose, further noted "a large wagon yard attached to the establishment, families traveling, and large teams, can at all times be accommodated…and [we] will spare no pains to keep good entertainment, and a quiet and orderly house."

Hotels knew their markets. Watson's Hotel, closer to the Statehouse, also marketed to ladies and families. Mr. Watson also advertised the nineteenth-century equivalent of Car2Go—hacks with experienced drivers and saddle horses in readiness at all times. Amenities, parking and location counted, just as they did in the following century.

2

DISTINCTIVE
NINETEENTH-CENTURY HOTELS

Among all the accommodation options available for visitors to Columbus in the nineteenth century, five stand out. Location, reputation and longevity make them distinctive. Four of them—the St. Charles, the United States Hotel, the American Hotel and the Park Hotel—are described below.

The Neil House (or Neil House Hotel) stands in a special category. It began as a tavern in the 1830s and lasted, in its final form, well into the twentieth century. The Neil House, one of the grande dames of Columbus's Gilded Age hotels, will be in the following chapter, as will other historic Columbus hotels that began in the late nineteenth century and continued for decades as important and elegant destinations.

One historian who gathered, organized and frequently wrote local history vignettes for newspapers fifty years ago was Myron T. Seifert, who knew early hotel history. His own work relied heavily on Alfred Lee, an earlier historian. Lee lived the early days of Columbus history and felt hotel keeping was more than a business. It was a profession much like being a doctor or a lawyer and required special skills to cope with a transient but important and official population: politicians. The needs of the legislature dominated early hotel business—especially before the 1830s, when the borough of Columbus became an official municipality. Civilization in Ohio and in Columbus was almost biblical. Like the old tavern that proclaimed out of the wilderness came the rose, great hotels had to rise in order for the city to succeed.

Though there were a number of hotels near the canal (the west edge of Main and Mound Streets), as canal traffic was eclipsed by the railroads and ceased to be a "genteel" mode of transportation, the better hotels now competed for business near the Statehouse. The canal basin area became a sort of seaport resort "frequented by sailors whose chief demand is for grog," according to Seifert. One street, nicknamed the Bowery, became the notorious place where the rich gathered to see the derelicts of the city fight and make spectacles of themselves. Some other hotels, even those not by the canal, were little more than gambling resorts.

The best hotels served huge portions of food with surprising variety. It was not uncommon for a dinner to offer two varieties of soup, two or three kinds of boiled meats, six or seven roasted meats and ten or more vegetables. Much, of course, relied on local game. Desserts might include three or four kinds of pie. Thanksgiving was a chance for hotels to show off, as will be seen later in sample menus at the Neil House and American House Hotels.

Hotels of distinction also had the best service. In a pre-electric era, galvanic batteries were used to ring bells, calling the clerk's attention to individual room needs. Above the registration desk was a rack of small, jingling bells connected by cords to individual rooms. Clerks paid attention to which bells rang and dispatched an energetic bellhop to investigate. Elevators did not make an appearance in Columbus until after the Civil War. Unless a traveler enjoyed a workout of climbing stairs with his or her luggage, he or she would hope there was a hotel porter. The best hotels employed a bootjack who was sent to the room of each newly arrived male to assist him in taking off his tall boots.

Most rooms were unheated. When the guest could no longer endure a frigid room, he looked for a stash of buckets with paper and kindling in a back hall and started a fire in the grate or the stove of the room. This, of course, was a risky situation, and one that the hotel discouraged by charging fifty cents for the privilege of starting a fire in one's room. It was better for patrons to avoid the charge and avoid the risk of a fire by relocating to the bar until they were ready for bed.

Bowls and pitchers of water were the only means of washing. Outhouses were in the alleys. Feather beds were found only in better hotels. Service, however, including liverymen who opened doors for patrons, was relatively common in the better hotels because workers relied on tips and not salaries.

The St. Charles Hotel

The St. Charles Hotel was described in an 1878 article as "a handsome and commodious, four-story brick building" at the northwest corner of North High and Gay Streets. The St. Charles was erected in 1859 by William Neil and his son-in-law, ex-governor Dennison. It was managed by Charles Elliott, who "at once infused new life into the house and its business." It was said that he never forgot a face, greeting weary travelers with a firm "shake."

St. Charles was actually a refurbished former boardinghouse that could accommodate approximately fifty legislators when the legislature was in session. The name "St. Charles" was also a decidedly better moniker than "Mrs. Benter's Boarding House." Business proved to be so good, even after the legislature ended for the season, that the owners decided it was worth the investment to attract the "commercial trade." They purchased property to the north, adding twenty-seven more rooms, including a ladies' parlor, and raised the height of the building to four stories. In addition, they enlarged the former boardinghouse to make a forty-foot front entrance on High Street,

The St. Charles Hotel was a refurbished former boardinghouse that stood on the corner of North High and Gay Streets and was the result of a partnership between William Neil and his son-in-law, former governor William Dennison. *Columbus Metropolitan Library Image Collection.*

enlarged the dining room, put up two iron fire escapes and carried the walls of the old building up two and half feet to put a cornice on the property.

With a total of ninety rooms and boasting all the modern conveniences, The St. Charles had thirty servants, desirable cuisine and an electric annunciator, a fancy name for electric bells. The knobs for the bells were located immediately over the beds in each room, so that in case of "sickness or burglars the occupant has only to raise his arm and press upon the knob to bring an ever-wakeful servant to his room." There were smoking, reading and writing rooms and "sample" rooms on the first floor where salesmen could display their merchandise.

THE UNITED STATES HOTEL

The United States Hotel, located on the northwest corner of South High and Town Streets, met its demise in 1907, when the F&R Lazarus Department Store began expanding to the north from its previous location across Town Street. Today, Lazarus itself is only a memory.

Where children gazed at animated Christmas windows and the famous "air curtain" door greeted shoppers, the United States Hotel once stood. The hotel had actually closed in the 1880s, but the building remained for another twenty years. In its final days, as the department store was taking shape, the old hotel of Civil War days was used for storage for Lazarus. Before that, it was a Busy Bee restaurant with apartments above. Though over sixty years old, the building was said to be in excellent shape. As it was being dismantled and the fixtures of the Horne Saloon on the first floor were moved, the joists of the floor above were revealed. Hand-hewn logs supported the building.

Opened in 1846, the hotel's first proprietor was Colonel Philander H. "Philo" Olmstead, a well-known Columbus resident, and its second was Robert Russell, a frequent and always entrepreneurial hotel owner. Olmstead advertised in May 1846 that he was treating his customers to "fresh Cucumbers, the first of the season." Lest cucumbers were not a big enough draw, Olmstead also advertised his hotel in the *Cleveland Herald*, the *Cincinnati Gazette* and the *New York Tribune*. Robert Russell generally advertised himself as the draw whenever he changed hotels. Russell did, however, add the *Scioto Gazette* to the list of newspapers that carried an advertisement for the hotel.

Listing this information acted as a notice to salesmen from Columbus and others who passed through. Salesmen were encouraged to drop by the hotel to make new contacts (they also drank), keeping the hotel relevant and important to the growth of Columbus business. The hotel was popular with rural visitors. Perhaps its most memorable proprietor was the eighth one, who also stayed the longest. The United States Hotel was remembered as a fine hostelry with great service. Successful proprietors and managers were held in high regard in the business world, as well as the social world, where they reigned supreme. It was sometimes said that, like a poet, a hotel proprietor was born and not made. Perhaps they were held in such high regard because, in addition to catering to a customer's needs, they also were affable, good natured, well informed and kept secrets.

The United States Hotel was run by L. Steenrod, Esq., a native of Muskingum County, which was known for its coal and iron. There, he ran a hotel in Athens, Ohio, even before passenger train service. Travelers to his establishment, the Brown House, made the arduous trip by stagecoach. They were rewarded with a royal reception. Steenrod came to Columbus in 1875, taking over the United States Hotel in a greatly expanded business from the one in Athens, Ohio. The hotel had seventy-five rooms with a capacity for 160 overnight guests, 20 staff members and "an unlimited capacity for restaurant service."

It was during Steenrod's career that Tennessee Claffin held court in the parlor of the hotel, flirting and telling fortunes. Claffin, the sister of Victoria Woodhull, was as controversial as Woodhull, who ran for president of the United States (the first woman to do so) in 1872. Together, they owned a stock exchange (the first women to own a brokerage) and a printing company (the first to print the *Communist Manifesto* in English) and advocated for the legalization of prostitution (possibly the first to publically advocate). Vivacious and engaging, Claffin was also rumored to be the mistress of railroad magnate Cornelius Vanderbilt. Many in Columbus stopped by the hotel to see her for themselves.

THE AMERICAN HOTEL

The American Hotel (sometimes known as the American House Hotel) operated from 1837 to 1895 at 87 South High Street, the northwest corner of South High and West State Streets. Because of its prominent location across from the Statehouse, in a time when Ohio governors had to find their own quarters, Governors Richard Bishop and Thomas Young lived there—even after they were no longer governors. Ohio governors stayed in hotels, leased houses or lived at their own homes if they were local.

The American House was frequented by Ohio legislators and city politicians alike and, therefore, attracted lobbyists and salesmen. In the 1820s, it also attracted gentlemen interested in adding to their charm and social skills by signing up for dance classes to learn the new quadrilles, contra dances, waltzes and Spanish dances.

Richard McCoy, a Columbus city councilman for more than thirty years, opened the hotel to the traveling public on December 11, 1837. He helped make his hotel a mecca for politicians based on both its location, one block from the Statehouse, and the amenity of its saloon. McCoy's goal was to give the public a style that was "not inferior to that of any other house West of the Mountains."

According to a story told by local historian Ed Lentz, McCoy was always up for a celebration. He wanted to celebrate the opening of the nearly finished hotel by breaking a bottle of whiskey on the chimney, but instead, he fell nearly three stories to the street below. He survived; the bottle of whiskey did not.

General Duncan MacArthur had survived St. Clair's defeat at the hands of Native Americans and the "rough and tumble" of national politics, but according to Lentz, he was almost bested by the porch of the American Hotel in the 1830s. The porch, covered in heavy snow, gave way above MacArthur, breaking almost every bone in his body. He stayed three more days at the hotel and then went home.

The hotel was three stories tall, with retail on the first floor and rooms above. The balcony that almost killed MacArthur ran across the top of the first floor. By 1845, the hotel had expanded to accommodate sixty to seventy more guests. At that time it was under the direction of a popular host, William Kelsey, who went on to a New York hotel after three years. Within his short proprietorship, Kelsey's fame was often noted. "Mr. Kelsey, of the American, serves up the first Green Peas of the season, on Sunday last. They were accompanied by new potatoes, all of which were the product of the garden of Mr. Mouree, at the Southern part of the city." Perhaps life in Columbus in 1844 was less exciting than can be imagined, or Kelsey went on to New York because he had an excellent publicist.

Perhaps the best known of the proprietors to today's Columbus residents was Colonel Eli Blount. He ran the hotel from 1866 to 1874; however, many may not know his name until they associate him with a grave site in Green Lawn Cemetery that draws a great deal of interest.

Eli Jackson Blount and Sara Tucker Blount were the parents of George Blount, who died in a tragic accident at the American House Hotel. The little boy was five years old and their only child. The *Daily Dispatch* carried the story on February 14, 1873, under the heading, "Terrible Accident! A Little Boy Falls Over the Stair Bannister at the American House and is Fatally Injured—His Death This Morning."

George (called Georgie by hotel patrons) was a great favorite of the many who frequented the hotel. He fell over the bannister from the second floor to the first floor, striking his head on a heavy stove hearth at the bottom of the stairway hall. He lingered in agony for seven days after the accident, despite the efforts of Drs. Loving, Smith and Frankenberg (all well-known Columbus physicians). The little boy had started up the stairs to retrieve something he had forgotten in anticipation of taking a carriage ride with his mother. He dashed down the stairs in the quickest way a little boy could—riding down the smooth bannister rail. The clerk in the office and the porter heard the crash. Both rushed to his side. Colonel Blount carried his son upstairs, where the child remained "until death relieved him of his suffering."

Though he was to be buried in Hillsboro, Ohio, near Mrs. Blount's parents, George was buried in Green Lawn Cemetery (section X, lot 3). As the story goes, the Blounts used a newly completed painting or photograph of their son to have his statue created to mark the grave. Almost full size, the little boy's statue sits on a draped chair, with one leg tucked under the other and toys in his lap.

Its lifelike size not only draws the attention of those who stroll the cemetery, but it also encourages some people to regularly leave little presents such as water guns, Pez candy dispensers, Hot Wheels, action figures, small pumpkins at Halloween, seasonal decorations and even scarves and hats. Georgie has worn OSU baseball caps, Mardi Gras beads and sun glasses. No one knows who (or how many people) gives the statue reverent attention, but the items remain for a short time before they are removed by cemetery grounds people. Wet hats and scarves could damage the statue.

Older residents remember that the back of the American Hotel was built by Colonel Blount to expand the dining room. He used bricks that came from the old State Lunatic Asylum (East Broad Street near Jefferson Avenue). The asylum burned down in 1868. The bricks and the addition would survive longer than the hotel.

HISTORIC HOTELS OF COLUMBUS, OHIO

The American House was known for its Thanksgiving dinners, which in 1879, included three kinds of soup (one called Sportsman's Broth), four types of baked and broiled fish, turkey, rabbit, venison, duck, lamb, chicken, ham beef roast, veal roast, pork roast, mutton, calf's brains, woodcock, oysters, lobsters, beans, rice, beets, potatoes (in a variety of ways), tomatoes, cabbage, parsnips, turnips, onions, three types of pudding, three types of pie, five types of cake, almost twenty different sauces for all the dishes offered, a variety of nuts and apples and coffee and tea.

The American House Hotel ceased operating as a hotel, but the front became stores. The back became rental rooms. The last of the hotel (though barely noticed by passersby) did not disappear until the 1990s, when the Riffe State Office Tower was built on the site. Some of Colonel Blount's bricks remained. Historian Ed Lentz commented, "As excavators cleared the corner, for a brief time the basement of the old American House appeared with its rough stone walls and the remnants of doorways leading nowhere. In a few days it was all gone, and with it went a piece of the past."

THE PARK HOTEL

In 1876, ground was broken for a new hotel on the former site of the Capital University Preparatory school. Additional frontage on North High Street and Goodale Avenue was used. The four-story building had a front door on Goodale Avenue and another on North High Street. The North High entrance became the ladies' entrance.

It has been said that a portion of the old university was kept as a tower, and the hotel was built around it. However, sometimes stories are taken from articles promoting the building ahead of construction. The story of the university tower, according to historian Terry Sherburn, may not be true. Sanborn maps indicate it was built to be an observation tower. He also related that the Park Hotel did not take its name from Goodale Park but for the private park at its own front door.

The Park Hotel opened in 1878. The outstanding feature was the private park on the hotel grounds. The owner, Fred Michel, spent over two years trading lots, amassing capital, remodeling the older university building and converting valuables into hotel bonds. The hotel was in an enviable spot for business, with "chariots" from Town and High Streets ready to direct guests

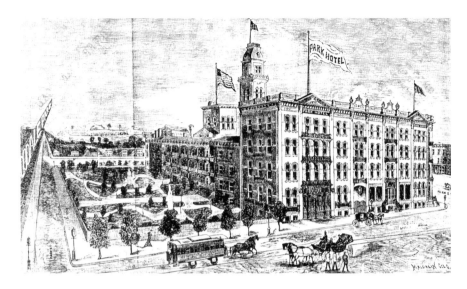

The Park Hotel opened in 1879. The building was unusual because it had a private park at the front of the hotel on Goodale Street. *Columbus Metropolitan Library Image Collection.*

there, a street railroad, a convenient location north of the Union Depot and the beauty of the nearby Goodale Park.

Photographs show the supposed tower of the former university building protruding from almost the center of the hotel. The building was in the Italianate style that was popular in Columbus, with an angled front, shops in the half-sunken basement, classical pediments and balconies. In addition, it had an elevator that not only went to the top floor of the hotel but to near the top of the tower, 105 feet up. From there, a circular stairway climbed higher, where there were two balconies from which to view the city. The hotel had 20 suites of rooms (each suite included a bed, a parlor and a bath) and 108 sleeping rooms. The rooms were supplied by an electric bell system, and there were even fire alarm bells in each room.

There was a bar, a billiard room, a barbershop, a magnificent dining room and reading rooms. The majority of the floors were marble, and the entire building was heated by steam heat. In 1905, under new management, it advertised "all outside rooms, good cuisine, an American Plan, a location with five car lines a day passing the door" and the fact that it "was the only strictly $2.00 per day hotel in the city."

3

THE GRANDE DAMES OF THE GOLDEN AGE
OF COLUMBUS'S HISTORIC HOTELS

In a full page advertisement in the *Old State Journal* on the morning of August 12, 1908, four of Columbus's downtown hotels joined forces to beckon to the well-heeled traveler: "State Fair Visitors Will Find a Welcome and Unexcelled Service at Either of These Four Leading Hotels." Never mind the slip in grammar, the drawing in the center of the page summed up the service, showing a man ordering from an attentive waiter. There is a tablecloth, a bottle of water and a small, artsy lamp. In each corner of the page, one hotel is featured.

The Chittenden Hotel was called "the most modern up-to-date 'American Plan' hotel in the United States." The Hartman Hotel offered "excellence, comfort, and enjoyment of rooms at moderate prices. Mid-Air Restaurant (coolest eating place in Columbus) at reduced prices." The Neil House advertised its "restaurant (Chef De Francais) guaranteed to be the only 'New York Style' restaurant at reduced Columbus Prices." The Southern Hotel was "fire proof and modern in all appointments, serving both 'American' and 'European' plans." These were the four elegant options for the Ohio State Fair–goer who had slugged through a muggy, humid Columbus summer day among the pig barns, hucksters, roasted ears of corn and pie competitions to take the streetcar back to a white-tablecloth world.

But the traveler to Columbus in 1908 had not seen the most elegant hostelry. It hadn't been built yet. Within a few years, Columbus would offer the Deshler. Then, the grande dames would all be in place.

THE NEIL HOUSE AND THE NATIONAL HOTEL

Clarence Darrow—the famous lawyer who played a major role in the Leopold-Loeb murder trial and the Scopes "Monkey" trial—was from Kinsman, Ohio. He had attended law school in Michigan for one year, but as was customary at the time, he "read law" with a Youngstown lawyer to learn the trade. In 1900, he borrowed money from friends to take the train to Columbus, hoping to pass the bar exam.

Having arrived in Columbus on a Saturday night, he spent the rest of the weekend not studying but drinking in the Neil House bar, where he met an equally gregarious man. They drank and talked, talked and drank. On Tuesday morning, Darrow awoke on the floor of a Neil hotel room. His drinking companion was asleep on the bed, and Darrow stumbled to the door to ask what day and time it was. He returned dejected.

According to Sidney Eisenberg, what happened next came from the memoirs of the late Judge Same Silbert, a Cuyahoga County Common Pleas Court judge, who got the story from Clarence Darrow and put it in his book *Judge Sam* in a chapter entitled "At Last I Tell a Secret Confided by Clarence Darrow."

Darrow's drinking buddy asked what was wrong, especially since Darrow had been so brilliant up until his mind grew fuzzy. Darrow replied, "I am brilliant, all right. I came down here to take the Bar examination on Monday and here it is Tuesday. I've lost my chance to become a lawyer. I'm Clarence Darrow, the biggest sap in Ohio."

The drinking companion pulled out a sheet of names from his pocket, remarking, "All is not lost, my boy. It appears that I am your Bar Examiner. Let me be the first to congratulate you. I hereby make you a lawyer in good standing in the State of Ohio."

And thus, perhaps the most notable lawyer in America in the twentieth century passed the bar at the bar of the Neil House.

The Darrow secret is illustrative of the Neil House's legendary role in the world of lawyers, politicians and government bureaucrats. Located across North High Street from 1822 until its final razing in 1980, five successive buildings (all of which were associated with William Neil) occupied the site.

William Neil's Tavern (1822–32) gave way to the National Hotel (1832–41), and later, the first Neil House Hotel (1839–60) was built on an adjacent lot. The second and third Neil House Hotels (1862–1925 and 1925–80) also occupied this prominent location. The National Hotel was important to the development of the Neil House Hotels that would follow.

Colonel John Noble opened a place of public entertainment, called a "hotel," on High Street across from the Statehouse. The lot and the building were owned by William Neil and had previously been used as a tavern. Colonel Noble called his hotel the National and secured the hotel as a stopping place for the stages of the Ohio Stage Company, the offices of which were attached. The National Hotel was fully furnished and promised to live up to the high expectations one might expect in a first-rate hotel.

The National Hotel was also owned by William Neil, who had made his reputation in managing stagecoach lines. Those who registered at hotels frequently found their names in the newspaper the next day. The towns listed reflect the range of the visitors' origins on a single day. In 1837, guests were arriving from Ohio towns like St. Clairsville, Somerset, Sandusky, Circleville, Canton, Springfield, Cleveland, Hamilton, Piqua, Dayton and Zanesville but also from Wheeling, West Virginia; New York City; Philadelphia, Pennsylvania; Vicksburg, Mississippi; and a variety of places in Kentucky and New Jersey.

The National was well remembered by an old Columbus resident in 1880. His description of a single side of High Street across from the Statehouse underscores the competition for business, the importance of hotels to the Columbus economy and the celebrity of the owners and proprietors:

> *The old fashioned sign post and sign I can remember as well as though I had seen them but yesterday. The "National Hotel" had on oval sign, with the proprietor's name and the name of the house. I presume that very few to-day can remember the leading houses and what was upon their sign boards. Next to the National came the "American" first opened by Messrs. Dresback & Kelsey, afterward Pike & Kelsey. Their sign was similar to the National. Next was the old "Globe"…and was kept by "Uncle Bob" Russell…a better man never kept a better hotel. His sign had upon it a globe. Next was the old "Lion Hotel" kept by J. Armstrong…upon his sign was a lion. Next was the "Union Hotel" kept by William Rose, where his son John D., obtained his first knowledge of the bar business and afterwards became the most celebrated bar-keeper in the United States, receiving for his service as head bar-keeper in the old St. Charles Hotel in New Orleans, La., the largest salary every paid a bar-keeper in this country.*

"The old citizen," as he called himself, continued to describe the many well-known "sporting men" and politicians who came to Columbus to stay and to socialize (sometimes for the entire season), "sitting in arm chairs under the awning on High Street, each with a large glass of mint julip [*sic*] very leisurely sucking it through a straw."

The first Neil House was a modest structure, but it was still impressive at a height of five stories. In 1839, William Neil began the construction, estimated to cost $100,000 (in 1839 prices). Prices contradict each other. It is said he paid the monumental price of $100 for the 212.5 feet of frontage. Others said the hotel costs were $21,250. Mythology and contradictions fit into all Neil House stories.

Colonel Philo Olmstead, who had been associated with the United States Hotel, became the proprietor. Neil, however, was no stranger to the hotel business. In addition to being associated with the National Hotel, he had once managed the Golden Lamb (in Columbus not the one that still stands in Lebanon, Ohio) for a short time in 1825.

William Neil and his wife, Hannah, had come to Columbus in 1818, and he quickly established a stagecoach line between Columbus and Granville, followed by others that connected to Worthington, Sandusky, Wheeling and Buffalo.

As early as the 1830s, when the city was still a teenager, the Neil House was attracting visitors from the East Coast and the South. And why not? Not only had the previous National Hotel been a draw, but now the Neil House was advertising fully operational baths ("a delightful luxury"). Warm, cold and shower baths were available at all hours—and, as if there could possibly be more, ladies' baths were available, and tickets could be obtained by ringing a bell in the ladies' parlor where a female attendant could wait in readiness. The early hotel had no internal bathrooms, but the outhouses in back were of solid black walnut cut from Neil's own woods.

Neil House amenities (not just baths and the solid walnut outhouses—it could have been the fresh Mackinaw trout) drew in almost two hundred guests every three days. Neil's enterprise also drew in other businesses. In one of the earliest references to the Neil House (1839), William Platt advertised he had removed his watch and jewelry shop from a previous location to the Neil House, where he had a new assortment of watches, jewelry, silverware, cutlery, lamp glass, perfumes, spectacles, flatware, Britannia ware and piano fortes. Just two years later, F. Bentz & Co. opened the Neil House Confectionary for the manufacture of their light, fancy teacakes.

In 1846, Neil and his wife left the hotel in a trust for their eldest son, Robert, who was to manage it for his siblings. It was to be held in a trust until the six Neil children died and then sold, with proceeds divided among the descendants of the children.

In February 1848, a fire broke out on the third floor, causing much damage to the roof and foreshadowing a more devastating fire that would happen twenty years later. Repairing the Neil, more businesses set up shop and advertised as being part of the hotel, like Thomas Butler, who advertised as the sole agent in Columbus for the sale of hernia trusses (useful, no doubt, to stagecoach riders).

The shop of L. Lesquereux & Sons was advertised as part of the Neil House, although it was really a neighbor of the hotel. It drew the best clientele, specializing in watches, silverware, perfumery, jewelry, clocks, canes and fancy goods. Lesquereux's materials came directly from Europe, especially Switzerland, his own place of origin. There, he had been a teacher, a paleontologist, a naturalist and a botanist. In Columbus, he corresponded with William Sullivant, a son of the founder of Franklinton and a noted botanist, and with Harvard University scientist Louis Agassiz, America's most well-known nineteenth-century scientist. But Lesquereux lived his quiet life as a jeweler in Columbus. His wife, a former countess who once had been his student and gave up her royalty to marry him, acted as his interpreter because he was deaf.

In 1858, Professor Fowler, a well-known "architect" and advocate of the octagon house style, used the hotel as his lecture site. He was best known as a phrenologist, explaining to audiences how the bumps on one's head could reveal much about a subject's personality, tastes, health and even future. He was at the Neil for nine evening lectures, willing to delineate people's characters with his own hands. He would, of course, see private patients for twenty-five cents. His advocacy for the advantages of eight-sided houses set off a small building boom of octagon houses in the Midwest and East. He believed that everything was better in an octagon house—fruit would not spoil as quickly, knives would not dull and marriage was better. Fowler liked to talk about marriage—the code word for "sex" in the nineteenth century.

English novelist Charles Dickens was one of the most famous Neil visitors. Most sources never relate that Mrs. Dickens accompanied him, but she did. His diary reveals that he arrived at seven o'clock in the evening in May and was "vastly pleased" with the hotel even though it was not

Even one hundred years later in 1940, the Neil House attracted businesses at its doorstep. This view of High Street looking south (with work in progress on the bricks around the streetcar tracks) includes Adam Hats and Rogers Jewelers. *Grandview Heights Public Library.*

yet finished. He referred to it in his *American Notes*, and "his few lines put Columbus on the map," according to Myron Seifert. He pronounced the hotel "pleasing," despite a bumpy stagecoach ride that left him bruised and sore.

Fifteen presidents of the United States and many presidential candidates registered at the hotel, though some are associated with the second Neil House. Andrew Jackson was the first, followed by William Henry Harrison, Abraham Lincoln, Andrew Johnson, Ulysses S. Grant, Rutherford Hayes, James Garfield, Chester Arthur, Grover Cleveland, Benjamin Harrison, William McKinley, William Taft, Teddy Roosevelt, Woodrow Wilson and Warren Harding. Stephen Douglas, Lincoln's opponent, stayed there, too.

In 1840, the "Log Cabin Campaign" for William Henry Harrison started with the Whig political party in Columbus. This led to the slogan "Tippecanoe and Tyler Too," referring to Harrison's defeat of the Native Americans at Tippecanoe and his choice of Tyler for vice president.

William Neil built a great canoe on a wagon and drove it in a parade with Harrison by his side. Henry Clay, who was from Kentucky, was a frequent guest to Columbus and stayed at the Neil on two occasions; the latter was "in state" as his body was sent through Columbus to be buried in his home state.

P.T. Barnum stopped at the Neil as well. In 1845, General Tom Thumb from England arrived by way of the American Museum in New York. He was, at the time, "the greatest curiosity in the world." At eleven years of age, he stood twenty-four and a half inches tall and weighed twenty pounds, with "beautiful black sparkling eyes and rosy cheeks." Columbus residents were invited to call and see "this novelty" as he was headed for the South. He was exhibited at the Neil House, room twelve, with admittance at twelve and a half cents per person. Jenny Lind, called the Swedish Nightingale for her beautiful voice, was a guest at the hotel. Ellen Terry, the English actress, stayed there with family as a seven-year-old.

Fifty years before a royal visit, Columbus hosted one of its most anti-royal visitors (however, see the entry on the Seneca Hotel, too). In 1852, Louis Kossuth stayed at the Neil House and spoke to crowds from the hotel balcony. Kossuth, the Hungarian revolutionary sometimes called the George Washington of the Hungarian people, was on a speaking tour of the United States to enlist his support for a democratic Hungary, free from the Hapsburg Empire.

He was led from the Union Depot to the hotel by a procession of legislators and the governor and was "followed by mechanical associations, benevolent societies, and a delegation of the city butchers on horseback." Kossuth was wildly popular wherever he went, and there is still a gold plaque in Columbus City Hall that marks the occasion of his visit. However, he could not say much. By the time he reached the Neil House, he simply was too exhausted, but he thanked the workingmen of the city who had taken up a collection for him.

It was well known that the Neil hosted the famous and the rich, but the hospitality extended further—sometimes. In 1845, in a letter to the *Ohio State Journal*, the writer lavished praise on the furnishings, staff and decorum of the hotel but concluded with an interesting story. Mr. Crowles, the accomplished host in the dining room, went out of his way (and demanded the same of his waiters) to make two men particularly comfortable as they sat down to breakfast. The men, judged to be laborers by their clothes and demeanor, appeared to be embarrassed by their surroundings. The letter writer noted that the staff immediately moved to offer the breakfast bounty in such a way as to make the men feel comfortable. He felt that added to the high character of the Neil House.

In 1879, the hotel restaurant advertised a Thanksgiving dinner to rival the one advertised at the American House Hotel the same year. In addition to all their offerings, the Neil Hotel offered pigs' feet, broiled quail on toast, spring lamb kidneys, chicken wings, lady fingers and five different pies but only one soup: oyster. The dishes were often listed by their French or New York names.

James Poindexter had his barbershop in the basement of the Neil House. If one saw his barbershop ad in the newspapers of the time, it would be easy to dismiss him as just another African American barber at a hotel—a man who needed to hustle to provide for his family, perhaps mixing flattery with the proper decorum that was expected from someone of his class in a white world.

But his story, because it is better known, may illustrate the "other" lives of nineteenth-century hotels. Poindexter was a barber and a minister who came to Ohio from Virginia at age nineteen, working to buy his family out of slavery. In addition to barbering, he served as pastor of the Second Baptist Church for fifty-five years. As a man who waited on the top politicians of his day, including captured Confederate generals and officers who were permitted visits out of Camp Chase, he and his colleagues were in a position to pick up hearsay that benefited his other passion: the Underground Railroad network in Columbus. Fugitives were hustled out of downtown by night in wagons, orchestrated by many of the black workers of the hotels and city hall, while others were "hidden in plain sight," working at the Neil House in menial positions.

The first Neil House's life ended in a spectacular fire in 1860 on the night of Abraham Lincoln's election. The fire originated in the rear of the upper story. The scarcity of water, the defects of the fire hose and the great height of the building combined "to give the raging element the advantage. It reached the front on High Street about midnight, and by four o'clock in the morning, every piece of timber in the building was consumed, and portions of the south side, and many of the partitions walls had fallen to the ground," according to the *Ohio Statesman* on November 11, 1860.

The loss was immense, though some furniture and valuable articles were removed. Fire companies from Cleveland and Cincinnati had been requested by telegraph, but the fire spread too quickly.

The second Neil House was a five-story brick building with a curved wall at the northeast corner. Sometime between 1892 and 1899, the well-known Columbus firm of Yost & Packard remodeled this building. It is this building that is most associated with the history of Columbus at the turn of the twentieth century. Looking back, when the second Neil House was getting ready for demolition in 1923 in anticipation of a new Neil House, President Warren G. Harding, a native Ohioan and frequent visitor to the establishment, called it "the real capital of Ohio." Well into the twentieth century, this Neil House remained the most tangible connection to the early history of Columbus.

William McKinley and his wife, Ida, lived in the hotel when he was governor of Ohio. Ida, an invalid, was well cared for in the hotel. They had a view of the Statehouse from their front room. Each morning before McKinley left to cross High Street for his office, Ida had a flower, a red carnation, sent up for his lapel. When he reached the Statehouse side of the street, he would turn and wave to her. If he was in his office (on the first floor of the Statehouse to the south of the front door) at 3:00 p.m., he would signal "I love you" by raising and lowering the window shade. He was devoted and solicitous, and when he was shot in Buffalo (later dying from the wound), his first words were, "Be careful how you tell Ida."

Though he was buried in Canton, Ohio, he had a grand monument in Columbus. Today, the statue of McKinley, surrounded by allegorical figures of urban and rural Ohio life and the text of his last speech in Buffalo, stands at the spot across from the Neil House where he would wave goodbye to Ida. Her red carnation became the state flower. When the statue was unveiled years after McKinley's death, Ida was sadly upstaged by the mobs who came to see Alice ("Blue Gown) Roosevelt, Teddy's eldest daughter (see the Hartman Hotel story).

In 1893, European royalty visited the Neil House. The duke of Veragua, Spain, and his family visited the largest city to be named after their distinguished ancestor Christopher Columbus. Columbus mayor George Karb offered them a gold key to the city that unlocked a richly decorated box that held an American flag. Governor William McKinley extended his hospitality as well.

Royalty was always welcome, but from the end of the Civil War to World War I, hotels often drew the color line at their front doors. Sometimes African Americans were welcomed guests, other times they were discouraged. In 1895, the Neil House clerks were a little taken

A view from the Ohio Statehouse grounds of the second Neil House, where William McKinley and his wife lived when he was governor. *Columbus Metropolitan Library Image Collection.*

back by what they believed no longer happened (they should have checked with the other hotels). A man from Kentucky stepped to the desk, asked for his bill and stated he would have to go elsewhere because a "colored man happened to have a seat at one of the tables in the dining room."

Once, a proprietor stood down six Kentuckians who demanded that an African American man had to be "bounced" from the dining room. They were told state law was strict, and the hotel proprietor informed them (no matter how vocal they became) that they should pay their bill and leave. He would not permit them to interfere in the running of his business.

In 1902, famed educator and lecturer Booker T. Washington arrived in Columbus to speak at the First Congregational Church. He was a frequent visitor to Columbus and planned to stay at the Neil House to work on his new book, *Work with the Hands*. His last stay in Columbus was at the Chittenden Hotel. Sometimes he stayed at a rooming house on West Eleventh Avenue owned by a member of St. Paul's AME Church. If Dr. Washington was part of a larger convention of black men, generally groups of ministers, some hotels chose to not have them all stay at one hotel, sending some on to other locations.

For the majority of African Americans who traveled to Columbus, if they did not appear to be famous or affluent, hotels might discourage them as room or dining guests. African American travelers might seek boardinghouses in black neighborhoods or find accommodations through black churches. One African American Columbus entrepreneur, William

Hotel managers were local celebrities, as seen here in a cartoon of Ben Harmon, an early manager of the second Neil House Hotel. Although the Neil did not refuse African American guests, the cartoon clearly shows the racial attitudes of the time. *Columbus Metropolitan Library Image Collection.*

Litchferd, opened his own hotel (90 North Fourth Street) specifically for black travelers.

In 1916, the three-story, brick Litchferd Hotel was nearing completion. It was considered the finest and largest accommodation for African American travelers in the country, exceeding other hotels in New York and Baltimore, both of which had greater black populations. It was Mr. Litchferd's dream to provide a place for those who had been discriminated against by Columbus hotels, and it is believed the hotel lasted until the 1930s.

Excitement revolved around the Neil House in unexpected ways. Occasionally, pigs ran amuck at the Neil House, escaping from their owners, though it is never made clear why some people brought their pigs to a hotel and why it happened so often.

On November 9, 1905, a steer escaped from the Union Stockyards herd as it was being driven south on Third Street on the other side of the Statehouse. In a panic, it impaled itself on the Statehouse fence on Broad Street. With a sizeable gap in its neck, it dashed north and then reversed direction, heading straight for the Neil House. By now the streets were crowded, and when it ran on the sidewalk, pedestrians and gawkers dove into the shops and lobby of the Neil with the steer in full pursuit. Now winded, the steer was subdued with a rope around its neck and led away to the slaughterhouse.

In 1901, the second Neil House was modernized. The old lobby of dark red and black furnishings was outfitted in reds, greens and golds. New high-power electric candles lighted the rooms. New carpets and private bathrooms were installed. Room thirty-nine, where politicians met to discuss campaign strategy, was replaced with a writing room, and the dining rooms were brightened with white and gold furnishings. No two rooms were furnished alike, including the choice of wallpaper.

The new thirty-three-foot bar was made of solid mahogany and had a marble top. Marble and French glass mirrors, the largest in the city, were at the back of the bar. A long-distance telephone and a telegraph (and a stenographer) were available. Modern elevators were installed, and all electric lights were now controlled by switches. The décor and the behind-the-scenes equipment updates in the kitchen and laundry would remain for the next twenty years.

The hotel was known for the black walnut chairs out front where the regulars sat. There was a protocol for who sat where, and if one sat down with a newspaper, the paper was to remain when the reader left. Down the

One of the many grand staircases of the second Neil House Hotel. Much of the walnut for the woodwork came from William Neil's farm. *Columbus Metropolitan Library Image Collection.*

street, the Southern Hotel was known for its high-backed rocking chairs with woven bamboo seats and large arm rests. There were about fifty chairs at the Neil, and politicians were not the only ones who used them. Columbus was a huge baseball town, and after the game, professional baseball players relaxed in the chairs to rehash the game. The chairs existed in an era when women would not have dreamed of sitting in them. Daniel Webster, Salmon Chase and other luminaries of American history sat in them. In anticipation of the closing to build the new Neil House, the chairs were given away to friends of the hotel. Today, one is owned by the Statehouse and is on display.

In 1923, the decision was made to build a newer, more modern Neil House to replace the old. Furniture, artworks and equipment from the hotel were sold, including the bedroom set used by the McKinleys that the hotel had preserved. All antiques were for auction—over 1,500 pieces. Many were made of ancient oak and walnut from Neil's own farm. The so-called whispering booths where political deals were made were also sold. The bar was sold, and some of it was made into furniture for those who wanted to own a piece of history.

In the days before the Neil House officially closed, stories were told, primarily by elderly men who remembered the rooms in which they

The Neil House, Columbus, Ohio.

Across from the statehouse, the second Neil House Hotel was an important institution of state government. President Warren G. Harding later reminisced that there were more deals brokered in the hotel than on the floor of the legislature. *Columbus Metropolitan Library Image Collection.*

gambled, drank or quietly met with a woman (room thirty-three seemed to be a favorite). As they reminisced, the men defied Prohibition laws (as they usually did) by drinking toasts of a stout rye.

There was a formal dinner at the hotel a few days before the doors were shut forever. A letter from an old Civil War veteran was read. He asked that someone might send him a momento and added, "If I come to Columbus, where can I go, now that it is passing?"

It was a question many asked on March 20, 1923. "Good Night, Gentlemen" was sung at the bar, and then Eddie, the bartender for thirty-three years, took off his bartender's apron, wrapped it up and with a "husky voice, half sobbed the old familiar dismissal: 'Bar's closed, gentlemen. Good night.'"

The third Neil House arrived in time to keep up with the boom times in Columbus during Prohibition. The new hotel was built in 1925 in a Second Renaissance Revival style, wisely using the former White Brothers shoe factory behind it for parking. While the first floor of the hotel was an ever-changing series of small shops, the second floor really carried the prominence of the building. Large, arched windows alternated with seven bays and fluted Doric columns. Classical architectural elements adorned the building on a grand scale. Substantial horizontal lines were

THE WHITE HOUSE

WASHINGTON

February 28, 1922.

My dear Mr. White:

I suppose my feelings, when I learned
that the old Neil House was to be razed and a great,
modern hotel placed on its historic site, were very
similar to those of every other Ohioan who has taken
any part in the state's public life in the last
generation or two. I am sure there is not one of
us but will indulge a bit of regretful sentiment
at realizing that the old house is to go. For so
many years that it antedates my own relations with
public affairs, and, indeed, I presume relations of
almost anybody now living, the Neil House might
fairly have been called the real capitol of Ohio.
On its lobby floor I first saw and felt the pulsing
movement of the political throng. If windows were
eyes, and walls had tongues, what a story the old
Neil House could tell of the public life of Ohio,
indeed, in no small way of the nation, for two
generations!

Every state capital with which I have
been familiar has had a leading hotel that has occupied
much the same relationship to the state's public life;
and in the case of the Neil House I am glad to know
that some effort is making to preserve this old history
of one of the most famous hostelries. Though I know
it is inevitable, I shall think of it going, giving way
to the march of progress toward better and more modern
things, with none but unfeigned regret.

Very truly yours,

Mr. Archibald White,
The Neil House,
Columbus, Ohio.

When the second Neil House announced it was going to be torn down and replaced with a grander hotel, many expressed sadness over the loss of the history. President Warren G. Harding's letter summed up the feelings of many. *Columbus Metropolitan Library Image Collection.*

created with the use of two "water tables," a frieze of windows and blue terra cotta ornamentation above the windows at the top, set off by cornices and stone balustrades. The third and final Neil House was a fine example of an early skyscraper.

It opened with a bang on August 25, 1925, with dinner, dancing and gifts for the almost eight hundred invited guests—bookends of the hotel and Neil House cigars. Thirteen stories held 657 rooms. By now, Columbus had taken on a new life. The devastating 1914 flood was resulting in a new civic center, city hall, police station and federal courthouse.

During Prohibition, according to David Gold, who wrote a history of the Ohio legislature, there were about one thousand speakeasies and beer flats and about four thousand bootleggers. That was actually a conservative number, since every bellboy and hotel attendant could produce good liquor on very short notice.

However, Prohibition changed the hotel in unexpected ways. The dining rooms suffered because of the availability of cheap liquor from the bootleggers. Hotels supplied mixers for the booze. The new popularity of football at Ohio State and the consumption of alcohol were a disaster. Hotel guests went wild. One year, the football goal posts ended up in the lobby.

The third Neil House was a popular subject matter for postcards from Columbus until its destruction in 1981. *Columbus Metropolitan Library Image Collection.*

The Neil House removed lobby furniture to protect it from destruction. Due to the changing times, hotels were forced to scale back fancy dining rooms because no one ate there. Instead, they opened coffee shops.

Four years after its opening in 1929, when Major Henry Neil, the last of the Neil children, died, a formal suit, which had been set up by the will of the trust in 1846, was filed to sell the Neil site. In 1929, the site was assessed at just under $3 million, about 110 times what William Neil had paid for the property. The ninety-nine-year lease on the property, held by Outhwaite & Linn, a Columbus legal firm, stayed in place. The money was distributed among forty members of the third and fourth generations. Including great-great-grandchildren, there were 132 descendants. Each of the six branches received an equal share.

In 1934, First Lady Eleanor Roosevelt, having taken the overnight train from Washington, D.C., to Columbus, was a guest on the eighth floor of the Neil. There were crowds of women in the lobby and more outside by the limousine that was waiting to take her to her speaking engagements. The presidential suite upstairs was filled with orchids, yellow roses and chocolates. She had come to speak on what the public expects of its teachers, and she promised it would be in a facetious manner.

In 1938, the Neil added a new feature: the Century Room. While called "the restaurant of tomorrow," its elegance seemed like an excuse to remind the public of the hotel's history, which it hoped would encourage more guests. The room was, in fact, never described, though there was a photo that showed a nightclub-like setting.

When World War II came, according to former hotel personnel, waiters left, doggie bags appeared on the table, the French chefs left the kitchen and the European Plan (which provided no food or "boarding") was adopted.

From 1925 until 1980, there were birthday parties observed for the Neil House itself. Old stories about the first and second Neil Houses were told. Even when other downtown hotels were closing after World War II, most assumed that the Neil House Hotel stood the best chance of transitioning into the twenty-first century.

The hotel appeared to weather the economic changes of the downtown area, even managing to secure a parking agreement in the 1950s with the Statehouse's creation of underground parking. The hotel would be connected to that parking garage by a tunnel, and it was now advertised as the Neil House Motor Hotel. The hotel corporation paid for the tunnel, but the term "motor hotel" did not help.

The lobby of the third Neil House had a striking resemblance to the lobby of the Great Southern with its open balcony. *Columbus Metropolitan Library Image Collection.*

The mezzanine lounge of the third Neil House was a popular meeting (and people watching) place. It was frequently used for political meetings. *Columbus Metropolitan Library Image Collection.*

Opposite, bottom: The dining room of the third Neil House was frequently used for banquets, private parties and political conferences. *Columbus Metropolitan Library Image Collection.*

While the hotel was quietly bleeding, life appeared no different to the casual observer. In 1955, the Neil House planned $500,000 in improvements in the bathrooms and air conditioning. A refurbished billiards room and coffee shop were planned. A banquet was held by the Columbus Bar Association to honor forty-seven members who had served actively for more than fifty years. The room was filled with luminaries, like Carrington T. Marshall, former Ohio chief justice and a presiding judge at the Nuremberg trials after World War II. One speaker talked about a lawyer who often came to court with "a snoot full" of alcohol in the morning and twice as much in the afternoon. Unabashed, he looked at the judge and said, "Your honor, if you think you're sober enough to continue now, I'm ready."

Columbus in the 1950s had a vice problem, and all the best and popular hotels kept a "house dick" (detective) on staff, mostly to be aware of events that needed to be covered up. It was well known that some Columbus police contributed to the criminal activities on the side. The Columbus vice squad acted undercover, and many stories did not make the newspapers but were widely known. Prostitution flourished in hotels, and several women catered to state legislators and their high-paying friends and lobbyists. One civic-minded working girl always cut her rates from fifty dollars to thirty dollars for state legislators.

House detectives checked on suspicious activity. When an old and well-known Columbus businessman, known to drink away his clients' money, began acting oddly at the Neil House, the hotel dick was sent to check on him. The man, who had friends in high spaces, appeared to have some of his financial problems solved after talking on the phone (to the governor, no less). But unable to raise the $5,000 he desperately needed, he walked to a lesser hotel and threw himself out the window. Presumably, he went to the other hotel because he had too much respect for the Neil.

Illegal poker games and gambling became other Neil House activities. Retiring legislators sometimes received a deck of cards as a parting gag gift to remind them of the good times (and it was much more acceptable than receiving a pair of panties to remind them of call girls).

One legislator commented that he could walk into the Neil House bar at 6:00 p.m. and see everyone he needed to see about a pending bill. Republicans and Democrats drank together, and there was a collegiality that transferred into bipartisanship. In the following years, that spirit simply did not transplant into other spaces when the Neil met its end in 1980.

In 1968, the Neil House Motor Hotel Company sold the property to Hotel Investment Company Inc., a Columbus-based corporation, the president of which was John W. Wolfe of the *Columbus Dispatch*. The hotel had been plagued with financial troubles, including a sheriff's sale, but conventions seemed on the upswing. The Neil House could handle over

THE NEIL HOUSE
"On Capitol Square"

One of the last Neil House Hotel logos. Marketing the Neil House as a "motor lodge" did not help improve business. *Columbus Metropolitan Library Image Collection.*

1,200 guests in the banquet room and had amenities such as the Town and Country Dining Room, the Red Lion Restaurant and a cocktail lounge. It also had over twenty leased offices and businesses, ranging from Trans World Airlines to the Ohio Trucking Association, a beauty salon and a hat shop.

There were plans to continue renovations and expand west to Front Street. The Front Street tract was formerly the site of the Wolfe Brothers Shoe Company, now occupied by the Wear-U-Well Shoe Company and the Capital Garage.

The staff at the Neil House breathed a sigh of relief when the hotel was purchased by a Columbus company, even though the hotel that was worth $7 million in 1925 could not sell for $1 million in 1968. William Dunn, Neil House general manager (see the Virginia Hotel for more information on the Dunn family), stopped worrying his hotel was about to be raised and a Datsun car parked where the newsstand was, according to James Scharff, writer for *Columbus Monthly* magazine.

In 1977, the Capitol Room was redecorated in a French country garden theme, and the Sonia Modes Trio was the new entertainment. The Red Lion was next on the list for a face-lift, despite the fact that it had been redone in 1965 and updated to include draft beer and buffet sandwiches at the same time the Caucus Room had been redone. Another new feature was "the hanging restaurant, presumably a terrace restaurant, not one associated with the Ohio Penitentiary."

In November 1980, the Neil House employees were notified that the hotel's final days would be in December. The Wolfe interests had been sold to Gerald D. Hinds, a Texas developer, and there were already plans for a forty-story Huntington Bank Headquarters to be built on the Neil site. Employees were stunned. There was no mention of severance pay or job placement help.

The Candlelight Dining Room in the Neil House was decorated in red; even the walls and ceiling were red. *Private Collection.*

One worker was quoted in the paper the next day: "I don't think anybody had any idea this place was getting closed up. I can only guess the big guys knew, because it was sure a shock to the rest of us." The news was delivered in a printed note, which led another employee and father of five children to state, "They could have at least stuffed us all in the ballroom and told us."

In the wake of the loss of the Union Station just a few years before, many felt that the city was changing because of what happened behind closed doors. After the Columbus Landmarks Foundation, formed after the demolition of Union State, met as a board, there was resignation to reality. Landmarks board president Henry Hunkler, a respected professor of geography at Ohio State, could only hope the replacement for the hotel would have a good design.

Ten minutes after the two o'clock checkout time on December 19, 1980, the last guest, Representative William Healey from Canton, left. On April 3, 1981, hundreds of shoppers lined up outside the Neil House for the start of the liquidation sale of the old equipment and furnishings. Chandeliers sold for $45 to $950. Juice glasses were $1.

The job of writing the Neil House obituary seemed to fall to the *Columbus Citizen-Journal*, perhaps at least in part because the Wolfe family interests that sold the hotel also owned the *Columbus Dispatch*. By November 18, 1980,

Despite all of the improvements on the interiors of the third Neil House in the 1970s, the hotel was still struggling to make a profit. *Columbus Metropolitan Library Image Collection.*

Interiors of the third Neil House Hotel after its last redecorating. The bottom picture is of the McKinley suite in 1975, even though McKinley had stayed in the second Neil House. *Columbus Metropolitan Library Image Collection.*

probably every adult and many schoolchildren could have recited the history of the Neil House and its famous guests because every local and national paper related the Neil House's history. The editorial farewell ended simply with the resignation many were feeling: "We will be sorry to see the Neil House go…a bit of Columbus as we have always known it, will go with it."

THE CHITTENDEN HOTEL

In the late nineteenth century, several serious hotel fires made headlines in central Ohio. Among them was the Chittenden Hotel, destroyed—not once but twice—by devastating fires. But from the ashes of the two Chittenden Hotels came scrupulous attention to the use of noncombustible materials and modern egress. The Great Southern Fireproof Hotel and the third and most glorious Chittenden Hotel were built with new technology.

Henry Treat Chittenden was a lawyer, real estate magnate and capitalist. Born in 1834, Chittenden's career covered many different fields. He was a graduate of Yale University Law School and practiced law in Columbus. But being a lawyer bored him, and he decided to pursue other interests, specifically real estate. In the 1880s, he owned the Columbus Railway Company (horse car), the predecessor to the streetcar. Before getting into the hotel business, Chittenden was one of the most successful real estate developers in Columbus.

Chittenden was also a patron of the arts and music. One of his hobbies was composing music. In 1888, he composed an ode that was sung by 1,500 schoolchildren to celebrate the Centennial of the First Settlement in Ohio, an exposition organized by the State of Ohio Archaeological and Historical Society.

Along with real estate and the arts, Chittenden dabbled in other ventures. He owned two short-lived Columbus newspapers: the *Times* and the *Monitor*. In 1876, Chittenden bought out other stockholders of the Columbus Railway Company because he was unhappy with the horse car service on High Street and did not have confidence his complaints would be taken seriously if he did not own the company.

Chittenden was married twice. His first wife, Helen, died in 1889 at age thirty-eight. His second wife was Catherine Mithoff (daughter of E.T. Mithoff, who also dealt in real estate). His son Campbell was a Spanish-

An early view of the exterior of the third Chittenden Hotel, distinctive because of its pagoda-like roof. *Columbus Metropolitan Library Image Collection.*

American War hero but apparently a novice car driver who once drove the new family auto into the plate glass window of the Lazarus Department Store, prompting Fred and Ralph Lazarus to leave it there with a sign, "Everything New Comes to Lazarus First."

Ben Hayes recalled in the *Citizen-Journal* in 1976, "Among Chittenden's real estate holdings was the 34 acre site of Olentangy Park. He bought the cottage at Point Pleasant, Ohio in which President U.S. Grant was born and had it moved to the State Fairground in Columbus. After being an exhibit for many year, the Grant birthplace was returned to Point Pleasant."

For such an entrepreneurial (and wealthy) family, the hotel business was a not-to-be-missed opportunity. In 1873, Chittenden bought the five-story Parker Building (northwest corner of West Spring and North High Streets). The building held offices and shops and included the offices of the local headquarters of the B&O Railroad; Walk-Over Shoes (selling union-made shoes for $3.50 to $4.50); All Leathers for All Weathers Company; and the Vogue Shop. It was a fairly unremarkable commercial building in a prime location on High Street.

Nearby theaters like the Metropolitan Opera House became even more popular because of growing middle classes and available discretionary income. Chittenden recognized the potential of his building, and in 1888, he announced plans to keep some of the shops on the ground floor but transform the rest of the building into a hotel with an additional two stories.

He spared no expense and appointed the hotel with the best furnishings, fixtures and decorations available at the time. The improvements cost $100,000, with an additional $122,000 spent on the furnishings. To put Chittenden's spending in context, historian and blogger D.A. Kellough explains this was "at a time when most workers earned less than $10 a week, a loaf of bread cost a penny, and you could get two pounds of bacon or two whole chickens for a quarter."

The extravagant spending and the timing could not have been better for the new hotel. Demand for more theaters resulted in construction of the new Park Theater next door, almost a guarantee of a steady stream of guests and dining customers, as well as customers from the nearby Metropolitan Opera House. A year after construction and conversion began, the Chittenden Hotel officially opened in 1889, but fate had other plans.

After operating for a little over a year with a steady amount of business, a fire broke out inside the Park Theater and spread to the nearby Chittenden Hotel, which completely destroyed both structures. Shortly after this fire, there was another fire on January 26, 1892, that burned down the entire Metropolitan Opera block. Columbus was in shock over the dual fires and the loss of the theaters and the newly opened Chittenden Hotel. The ruins left a void and quickly created a demand for both a new hotel and theater.

Chittenden, though reeling from his bad luck, planned for a new hotel on the south side of the earlier one, with a theater directly behind it. Almost as soon the rubble of the first hotel was cleared, construction of the second hotel (designed by George Bellows Sr. and father of artist George Bellows) began. A new theater, the Henrietta—named in honor of his late wife, Helen—was also built. The Park Theater was also quickly rebuilt, along with a nearby auditorium replacing the Metropolitan Opera House. All the new buildings were reported to have the "new, safe and improved" electric ignited, gas jet lighting.

On November 25, 1892, the second Chittenden Hotel and the Henrietta theater opened to the delight of Columbus citizens. The Park

Designed by George Bellows Sr., this is the second Chittenden Hotel, pictured here before its destruction by fire in 1893. *Columbus Metropolitan Library Image Collection.*

Theater was yet to come, and the opening of an adjacent auditorium was delayed by litigation.

This hotel became a Columbus landmark known for its excellent food and service. Again, Chittenden outdid his competitors and spared no expense on the finest appointments and furnishings. Newly sworn in as Ohio's thirty-ninth governor, William McKinley and his wife, Ida, were so impressed with the hotel that they took up residence in a special four-room suite in the Chittenden Hotel.

Almost a year to the day after its opening on the evening of November 24, 1893, a fire broke out in the attached Henrietta before the eyes of the audience. The theater was safely evacuated, but the fire spread quickly. As fire crews arrived to battle the raging inferno, a strong wind fanned the flames, and the hotel and the Park Theater caught fire. All hotel guests were led to safety; however, Harvey Thompson of the hotel maintenance staff and a fireman died. All three structures were completely destroyed by fire, with a loss of approximately $1 million. The fire was, at the time, the largest and most destructive fire in the city's history. It also claimed the Princess Skating Rink and the Globe Museum north of the hotel.

Governor McKinley and his wife escaped harm with the other guests, but most of the possessions in their suite were lost in the fire. They relocated their

The charred remains of the second Chittenden Hotel after the devastating fire in late November 1893. The fire began in an adjacent theater and spread to the hotel, consuming the entire block. *Columbus Metropolitan Library Image Collection.*

official residence to a suite in the Neil House Hotel, where they would remain until Governor McKinley was elected into the White House. Newspapers incorrectly reported that the governor was out of town in Boston and that friends had rescued all of his possessions.

Years later, actor Arthur Bryon recalled that when the fire broke out in the theater, the ushers evacuated the guests, but no one told the actors backstage. The leading man appeared on stage and thought he had gone mad because the theater was empty. "I wondered about my sanity as I stood there in the middle of the stage," Byron recalled in 1907. "I crossed the stage and flung open a door. Flames leaped at me. Two city firemen then appeared and shouted that I leave." Bryon alerted his fellow actors backstage who were still unaware of the fire.

The old saying "Third time's a charm" may have crossed Chittenden's mind. Undeterred by his bad luck and determined to fulfill his dream of having a world-class hotel, he rebuilt. Kellough wrote:

Chittenden could have walked away. He was 59 years old, no longer a young man. The hotel had not been insured and Chittenden had seen $300,000 of his own money go up in the blaze. He had a loving family and a lifetime of accomplishments to take pride in. He still had plenty of money...He ignored the reasons not to and plowed into the work...There would not be a third fire. The new Chittenden Hotel would be as fireproof...Chittenden decreed "No wooden structural elements."

Nicholas Court was one of the early managers of the third Chittenden Hotel. He held this position concurrently with the management position at the Normandie Hotel. *Columbus Metropolitan Library Image Collection.*

Instead, the third Chittenden Hotel was built with brick, concrete, stone, tile and steel. With the destruction of the second Chittenden Hotel, a group of South Side businessmen saw an opportunity to redirect business growth back to the south end of downtown.

They built on the growing public fear of fires in hotels and theaters. Architects and building contractors (along with insurance companies and advertisers) developed new construction materials and methods to erect fireproof structures. Plans for a hotel and theater, discussed years before but never materialized, became a reality with the formation of the Great Southern Fireproof Hotel and Opera House Company. This time, Chittenden had some new competition.

The new Chittenden was rebuilt on an elaborate scale, designed by Yost and Packard and under the management of Joseph Shoup, to whom Chittenden would later sell the hotel.

Like the proverbial phoenix, the hotel had the architectural character that marked the Yost and Packard style—Moorish towers and overhangs, a series of Spanish turrets and stone rosettes. It opened to the public on March 16, 1895, regarded as one of the largest and handsomest hotels in Ohio. It contained over three hundred guest rooms.

The third Chittenden Hotel was even more luxurious than the first two—or any other hotel Columbus had ever seen in early 1895. "Fourteen railcars of Vermont marble were required for floors and wainscoting.

The lobby of the third Chittenden Hotel. *Columbus Metropolitan Library Image Collection.*

An early view of the lavish Chittenden Hotel dining room under an elaborate dome. This is the third Chittenden. *Columbus Metropolitan Library Image Collection.*

Nearly $20,000 in Turkish rugs and carpets decorated the floors," described Kellough, "Mahogany was imported from Honduras for the paneling in the bar. Marble, fine wood, brass, silver, mirrors, art glass, and elegant furnishings…Tasteful sculptures and beautiful paintings…The first floor restroom was such a luxury spot that it was written up in the newspapers!"

The Chittenden catered exclusively to wealthy clientele when it opened. It was well known for its excellent food prepared by European chefs, but the hotel was remembered the longest for a popular eatery called the Purple Cow.

In 1953, the Chittenden Hotel was bought by Chicago-based Albert Pick Company and became a sister hotel to the nearby Fort Hayes Hotel. The two hotels shared staff and resources for many years.

Much like other downtown hotels, the Chittenden was not immune to the declining hotel business in the 1950s and '60s. Upkeep on the ornate exterior of the hotel proved to be too costly, and most of the distinctive Spanish turrets, Moorish towers and overhangs were removed. The goal was to concentrate on maintaining the interiors of the aging hotel and save costs at the expense of the exterior appearance.

Also in 1953, a project was announced that would intersect with the future of the hotel for decades to come. The most ambitious building proposed to be built in Columbus (and never built) was the Temple of Good Will, a

CHITTENDEN HOTEL

COLUMBUS, OHIO

TURKISH CORNER

MEZZANINE FLOOR

The mezzanine and Turkish relaxing corner of the third Chittenden Hotel. Turkish corners in hotels and private homes were popular features before World War I. *Columbus Metropolitan Library Image Collection.*

CHITTENDEN HOTEL

COLUMBUS, OHIO

MUSIC ALCOVE

ENTRANCE TO MAIN DINING ROOM AND FRENCH ROOM

Interior views of third Chittenden showing the music alcove and the entrances to the French Room and the main dining room. *Columbus Metropolitan Library Image Collection.*

A postcard of the exterior of the third Chittenden Hotel in the 1940s. *Columbus Metropolitan Library Image Collection.*

building designed to be taller than the LeVeque Tower (American Insurance Union Citadel), which would serve as headquarters for all the Protestant denominations of the United States.

The site had already been purchased and covered two city blocks facing the Scioto River between West Long and West Spring Streets. As soon as an additional $330,000 (of the needed $750,000) could be raised, construction would start for conference spaces, hotel accommodations, a library, broadcast facilities, office space for five thousand workers and parking for 2,500 cars—estimated cost $20 million.

Why Columbus? Reformed, Methodist, Presbyterian, United Brethren and Quaker Church leaders had been convinced by Dr. B.F. Lamb, president of the Ohio Council of Churches, that Columbus was ideally located as the center for two-thirds of the country's population and that the country was ready for such a grand gesture of post–World War II Christian fellowship.

By 1968, as downtown real estate properties fell, the dream began to dissolve. The Ohio Council of Churches voted against making Columbus its headquarters. The net worth of the property (that now included the Smith Shoe factory, lots east of the factory and the Chittenden Hotel) was valued at $3.5 million and included city-donated property, including Marconi Drive.

Now it was a scandal. The State of Ohio offered $1,750,000 for the site on October 8, 1965, to build a new Ohio Historical Center, but

An exterior view of the third Chittenden Hotel in 1959. *Grandview Heights Public Library.*

Lamb dismissed the offer. Within three weeks, he changed his mind, but the state had already decided to build a new museum at the Ohio Expositions Center near the fairgrounds. The site was sold in December to Nationwide Insurance for $1,750,000—later revealed to pay off mortgages held by Nationwide, including for the Chittenden Hotel and other properties.

A view of the upper portion of the Chittenden Hotel in 1961, showing scaffolding along the top floor for the removal of the eaves. *Grandview Heights Public Library.*

The hotel went into receivership as part of the failed Temple of Good Will project in the early 1970s. Much the same story as its sister hotel, the Fort Hayes, the Chittenden Hotel was purchased by Nationwide Insurance and closed on March 15, 1972. That day on the front page of the *Columbus*

This photo shows construction scaffolding going up to remove the ornate exterior of the third Chittenden Hotel. *Grandview Heights Public Library.*

Dispatch, reporter Melanie Croker interviewed Hazel Gilbert, an elderly employee who had been the room clerk since the 1950s and whose final duty that day was to account for all the keys.

"It's funny how you get attached to a building. But you sure do," Anna McIlwaine, an elderly resident said. She and forty other residents were in the process of leaving.

The Chittenden, like many other downtown hotels, struggled in the decades after World War II. *Columbus Metropolitan Library Image Collection.*

A view of the Chittenden Hotel and the May Drug Company from West Spring Street in 1938. *Grandview Heights Public Library.*

A ghostly photo of the lobby and registration desk area of the soon-to-be-demolished Chittenden Hotel in 1973. *Grandview Heights Public Library.*

The building was demolished in February 1973. Today, the William Green Building, headquarters of the Ohio Bureau of Workers' Compensation, is on the site of the Chittenden Hotel.

THE GREAT SOUTHERN FIREPROOF HOTEL

At the turn of the last century, Columbus had thirty-two hotels, virtually all downtown. Some were well known into the twentieth century, like the Chittenden, the Deshler, the Neil, the Hartman and the Normandie. A few were the nineteenth-century hotels and taverns previously mentioned. Some were almost forgotten, but the buildings existed in some form into the twenty-first century—like Smith's European—and some were better known, if for no other reasons than for their unusual names, like the Stag Turkish Bath and Hotel.

But of all of them, only the Great Southern Fireproof Hotel (now known as the Westin Great Southern Hotel or Westin Columbus) remains as a

A delivery wagon, streetcars and a lone horseless carriage clatter past Smith's European Hotel, 6–10 East Broad Street. Smith's European Hotel became most associated with Roy's Jeweler and lasted well into the twentieth century. *Columbus Metropolitan Library Image Collection.*

The exterior of the Great Southern Fireproof Hotel shortly after it opened. *Library of Congress.*

hotel and is the city's oldest operating hotel (almost continuously since 1897) despite a few near-death experiences.

Designed by the well-known architectural firm of Yost and Packard, the hotel opened on August 23, 1897, and included the Southern Theater, Columbus's only remaining nineteenth-century theater, which had opened one year earlier. The Southern was the first fireproof hotel in Columbus.

The story of the Southern begins with the misfortunes of the Chittenden Hotel and an opportunity for several German businessmen on the South Side who were concerned with the growth of the city to the north. Streetcar lines carried travelers northward toward the Ohio Agricultural and Mechanical College (Ohio State) and eastward to new areas like Broad Street, Franklin Park and Bryden Road. With the growth pattern of the city moving up North High Street and a strong businessmen's lobby for the area above the old North Graveyard, German businessmen who were heavily invested in real estate wanted to direct the city's prosperity to the south of the Statehouse.

They saw the perfect time and opportunity to spring into action and build their own hotel and theater. But it had to be something different, something that would ease the fear of fire that was still fresh on people's minds. Investors formed the Great Southern Fireproof Hotel and Opera House Company, buying shares at a face value of $100 each. Nicholas Schlee, a brewer, was president of the company; Allen Thurman, vice-president; F.J. Reinhard, treasurer; and J.P. Bliss, secretary. Board members included George Hoster, Emil Kieswetter and Ralph Lazarus. Bliss later became the manager of the Great Southern Hotel. The theater was designed by the local architectural firm of Dauben, Krumm and Riebel. The hotel was designed by Yost and Packard, with fireproof materials of tile, brick, iron, steel and concrete. Construction began in 1894; the theater opened on September 21, 1896, with a production of *In Gay New York*.

The attendees were the rich and famous of Columbus: George Backus, Columbus's own theatrical celebrity; Dr. and Mrs. Hartman; F.O. Schoedinger; and the Ketchams, who sat in the first box on the right where Mrs. Ketcham, resplendent in a white brocaded satin gown, could show off the diamond trim of her dress. There was a curious lack of pre-theater parties; presumably, they would happen when Lillian Russell appeared the following week.

The grandeur of the Great Southern Theater, designed by M.S. Detweiler and Company of Columbus, gave an effect of warmth and elegance. The bright lobby was decorated with handsome portraits of theater celebrities, and the foyer was furnished with potted palms.

But it was the auditorium itself that stole the show—an electrified arch began at the stage opening and radiated to the balconies "to throw the sound waves from the stage to the remotest corners of the auditorium with equal distinctness." A whisper from the stage could be distinctly heard in the most remote areas of the auditorium. There were few theaters in the entire country that could surpass its beauty or architecture. The theater's greatest production was *Ben Hur*, with a cast of 250, a water battle, the chariot race and eight horses galloping on a hidden treadmill.

The Great Southern Fireproof Hotel opened on August 23, 1897. Many accounts of its elegance, lavish appointments and splendor filled the newspapers. The Great Southern was the poster child of the Gilded Age in Columbus, offering 250 rooms, with 50 having their own private baths—a very unique feature in 1897. The exterior's decorations were more muted, consisting mostly of terra cotta embellishments.

The original ballroom was located on the seventh floor with landscape murals on the south wall. Today, the ballroom is situated on the mezzanine. This was actually the original dining room of the hotel. Adorned with white

Decorative plasterwork above a doorway is shown in this 1983 close-up at the Great Southern Hotel. *Grandview Heights Public Library.*

marble, gold-painted cornices and stained-glass motifs of shellfish, poultry and other animals, it is reminiscent of the popular Victorian subject matter on dining room sideboards or in paintings of a bountiful feast—sometimes referred to as "death in the dining room."

The hotel's early eating and drinking establishments were well known and beloved, like the Oyster Bar and the rooftop beer garden where President McKinley and his cabinet held court when visiting Ohio's capital city.

Emil Ambos, son of a wealthy Columbus industrialist and candy maker, spent much of his bachelor life pursing his hobbies of fishing and camping. Though he died in 1898, he had set up a trust for an elaborate banquet for his fishing buddies, with any funds remaining to be given to the Children's Hospital. In 1901, an elaborate dinner in the Great Southern Hotel's banquet room transformed the space into a campsite with life-sized trees, pitched tents and pools stocked with fish.

The Southern produced its own electricity, had its own water supply from three wells in the basement and made its own ice. Heat came from huge, coal-fired boilers in the basement. In later years, the boilers were converted to natural gas. The theater had a rudimentary cooling system popular at the time (though seldom seen in Columbus except in some very wealthy homes). Ice was packed into a bin in the basement, and a large belt-driven fan forced the cool air through ventilating holes under the theater seats.

With all the technological achievements and lavish accommodations, the hotel sailed into troubled financial waters in 1900, clouded with an uncertain future almost from the day it opened. Poor choices and mismanagement created cost overruns. Less than three years after it opened, the company could not cover operating costs.

In an era of trusts and financial tycoons, talk of takeovers were frequent, and real estate development, always based on speculation and the markets, made real estate and development spectator sports. On January 10, 1900, it was announced that the Neil House Hotel, the Chittenden Hotel and the Great Southern Hotel were being consolidated into the Columbus Hotel Company. But the debt of the Great Southern Hotel turned out to be unappealing to investors.

Despite $300,000 cash on the table and some big names like brewer Nicholas Schlee, the deal did not go well. The partners in the trust stood to lose a great deal of money if the deal fell through, and it was rumored that the Great Southern was already leaking money and might foreclose.

As the song says: "you've got to know when to hold 'em/know when to fold 'em." The Great Southern decided to "hold 'em" at the behind-the-

A photo of the exterior of the Great Southern Fireproof Hotel taken in the early twentieth century. *Columbus Metropolitan Library Image Collection.*

scenes insistence of Ralph Lazarus, a Great Southern Hotel trustee. He politely repeated, "No deal." The others lost their appetite for the fight and said they had only been trying to save the Great Southern but did not care to be in the position of "begging to be sold a dead horse." They waited for the demise of the hotel to pick it up at a cheaper price. One hundred years later, the Neil House and the Chittenden Hotel have disappeared, but the "dead horse" continues to exist.

In 1900, the Great Southern Fireproof Hotel and Opera House Company was forced into receivership by a foreclosure. It was reported that building the hotel and theater cost $1.5 million, but the appraisal value was set at a staggering low $175,000 plus a lien of $180,000. In December, the hotel was put up for auction, but there were no bidders. The property again went up for auction on August 16, 1901. This time, both the hotel and theater were sold to Fred and Ralph Lazarus for $235,000. Things were looking up.

The Great Southern Hotel's rooftop garden was a combination of elegance and German tradition (this was, after all, a very German establishment) and made drinking beer while viewing Columbus from the top of the Southern very popular. However, the smokestacks of the

A lounge on the second floor of Great Southern overlooking the lobby. *Columbus Metropolitan Library Image Collection.*

The rooftop garden no longer exists at the Great Southern Hotel but was a favorite meeting place of President McKinley and his cabinet when he visited Columbus. *Columbus Metropolitan Library Image Collection.*

A historic photograph of the lobby of the Great Southern Hotel; today's Westin Great Southern retains much of the elegant style of the late Victorian era. *Columbus Metropolitan Library Image Collection.*

From left to right: Mary Agnes Thurber, mother of James; Millicent Easter, director and public relations person for the Southern Hotel; and Mrs. Thurber's sister-in-law, Mildred Fisher. This photo was taken in 1952. *Grandview Heights Public Library.*

hotel caused the guests' clothes to smell and their eyes to water. The rooftop garden lasted only a few years and then closed. The rooftop garden was a popular fad in New York at the turn of the twentieth century—it made sense in stifling summers, but it seemed so delightfully bohemian. New York's Waldorf-Astoria spent $50,000 a year on flowers for its rooftop garden, and patrons sat among ivy-covered pergolas and cascades of honeysuckle. The Southern Hotel's rooftop garden was decorated with electric lights strung from poles, the requisite greenery and the occasional presence of President William McKinley and members of his cabinet.

Along with visits from President McKinley, President Theodore Roosevelt also was a guest at the hotel. (He went to the Hartman Hotel on another visit.) It is said that President Roosevelt declared that the hotel sauna was his favorite in the country.

Of all the grande dames mentioned, only one of them—the Westin Great Southern Hotel—remains a downtown hotel; because of this, it holds a special place in Columbus history. The Southern is important for other reasons: it made a statement about the prosperity and importance of the German community, who saw themselves as now being part of the movers and shakers; it had a rooftop beer garden that brought a traditional German drinking custom into the mainstream; and it had a gimmick—the oyster bar.

An oyster bar was the foodie gimmick of its day and is worth mentioning because what started as a simple fare in the East to accompany drinks grew into an obsession in Columbus. If rooftop gardens were literally and metaphorically on the top of a hotel's draw, oyster bars were in the basement in the nineteenth century—the oyster cellar. An oyster house, oyster bar or oyster cellar served nibble bar food. Oyster madness took over America in the 1880s. Annual consumption of oysters in America was 660 oysters per person.

An oyster bar in a hotel implied extravagance and technological advances of the Gilded Age. Oysters would be shelled, packed in milk containers and shipped to Columbus, where they would be placed back in the half shell—the freshness was dependent on the timely arrivals and departures of the railroad, and year-round availability of ice was becoming less a novelty because of improvements in refrigeration. Imported fresh (or hopefully fresh) oysters from the eastern seaboard were delivered to Smith's European Hotel on the corner of Broad and High, and the Great Southern Hotel, the two most visited oyster bars in Columbus.

In the 1930s and '40s, the hotel was still a dignified and appealing hotel to visitors. It also rented suites, often to the elderly who could afford them.

The Great Southern Hotel lobby at Christmas, circa 1900. *Columbus Metropolitan Library Image Collection.*

The mother and brother of James Thurber, Columbus's favorite son and humorist, lived here, and he had made a name for himself in New York and even had his play *The Male Animal* debut in Columbus. He frequently visited family here. Mrs. Thurber, however, was a handful. She liked to play act, feigning fainting in the dining room to draw attention to herself and away from the bill. She would call out, "Ever see eggs fly?" And then toss a carton of eggs over her head (the carton was empty).

Former first lady Eleanor Roosevelt maintained fond memories of the Southern from her visits in the 1930s. On December 17, 1958, Mrs. Roosevelt, recently returned from a trip to Russia, felt Columbus was important enough to warrant her making a speech. She chose the Southern Hotel to address the American Association for the United Nations on the topic of the United States, the Union of Soviet Socialist Republics and the United Nations.

She was not the first first lady to visit the Southern. Decades earlier, Florence Harding had accompanied her husband, Warren, to Columbus, where he served as state senator and lieutenant governor. They lived together at the Great Southern Hotel when the legislature was in session, and she accompanied him to the legislature and social events. Warren still managed to cut out of smoke-filled poker games for unmentionable dalliances with Columbus's demimonde women.

Like many of the other downtown hotels, the Southern saw business drastically decline after World War II. The hotel went through several different owners but managed to stay in business. The downtown theater business also declined, and the attached Southern Theater also fell on hard times. By the 1960s, the theater had been reduced to country western concerts.

By the 1960s, the area around the Southern had changed. There were adult bookstores and topless bars across the street. This also attracted a number of gay bars that were forced to stay under the radar. Many storefronts were empty.

In 1969, the Lazarus family interests sold the hotel and theater to realtor Robert Weiler Sr. An article in the *Columbus Dispatch* on July 13, 1969, stated that the new owner would renew a long-term lease with the New Southern Hotel Company for the continued operation of the hotel. The Weiler Company also considered turning the hotel into an apartment building. Some attempt was made to create apartments on the sixth floor, and drawings exist showing the hotel as an apartment building and the theater transformed into a parking garage.

Marion Fisher, art coordinator, and Greg Swartz, general manager, confer in the ballroom of the Great Southern Hotel in 1985. *Grandview Heights Public Library.*

In 1974, the hotel and theater were sold to William R. Mnich, who hoped to see the building restored. Though Mnich had a passion for the building, previous improvements had only been cosmetic, and the heating, plumbing and electrical systems were patched rather than replaced.

The building was slated for closure, and its china, equipment and furnishings were already on display on tables in the main lobby. Shoppers were heading in the doors when the hotel's stay of execution came. In 1982, the hotel and theater were purchased by Bill and Barbara Bonner and David and Vicki Brooks, who restored the hotel to its original condition. All of the mechanical systems were replaced, and the façade was restored. Today, the hotel looks much as it did at the turn of the century, and it is perhaps the "greenest" hotel in regard to the environment.

The Southern Theater was donated to the Columbus Association for the Performing Arts (CAPA) in 1987 and was subsequently fully restored to its original elegance and reopened in 1995. In 1997, the hotel became part of the Westin family under the Starwood Inc. collection of international fine hotels and properties. In 2006, the Marcus Corporation purchased the hotel, kept the Westin brand and embarked on another multimillion-dollar renovation. The hotel and theater are listed on the National Register of Historic Places.

THE HARTMAN HOTEL

The building on the northwest corner of Fourth and Main Streets was built in 1898 as an elegant office building and headquarters for the Pe-Ru-Na Company. Designed by architects Kremar and Hart, the building is an excellent example of Neoclassical architecture and would later become the celebrated Hartman Hotel.

Dr. Hartman was the richest man in Columbus from the early 1890s until he died at age eighty-eight in 1918. Hartman built his fortune from a "cure all" tonic named Pe-Ru-Na (or Peruna)—the formula for which Hartman claimed he had received in a dream from an Indian. Pe-Ru-Na was the bestselling patent medicine in the country starting in 1887.

Because of the popularity of his product, many knew Columbus as "Peruna City." James Harvey Young, an expert on the Hartman empire, described the huge impact Hartman's product had in American society: "Although Pe-Ru-Na was promoted to cure only catarrh, the millions of brochures and

Hartman Hotel, Columbus, Ohio.

Above: Originally intended as an elaborate office building and company headquarters, the Hartman would shortly evolve into one of the most lavish hotels in Columbus. *Private Collection.*

Right: Billy Ireland's cartoon of Dr. Hartman showed the many interests and businesses he was involved in. *Columbus Metropolitan Library Image Collection.*

almanacs Hartman issued and his extensive newspaper advertising defined catarrh as encompassing all ailments known to humanity. By the new century, Pe-Ru-Na was the most widely advertised—at $1 million a year—and the bestselling proprietary medicine in the nation."

At the height of its popularity, testimonials (paid for) rolled in from Civil War generals (both sides), actors and congressmen. Babies were even named after it. But others, like Columbus's Dr. James Baldwin, founder of Grant Hospital, remained skeptical. Even when passage of the Pure Food and Drug Act of 1906 revealed that the product contained 27 to 30 percent alcohol, it did not deter much of the product's popularity. According to Young, Hartman studied medicine for a term in 1852 at Farmers' College near Cincinnati, took a two-year apprenticeship and studied at Cleveland Medical College. By 1857, Hartman was a medical doctor, though his certification was bogus.

At the time of his death, his holdings included the downtown factory and elegant administration building, decorated by Tiffany & Co. (Third and East Rich Streets); the Hartman Office Building and Hartman Theater (Third and East State Streets); the Hartman Hotel (South Fourth and Main Streets); the Hartman Surgical Hospital (Fourth and Cherry Streets); and his grand marble mansion (East Town Street and Washington Avenue).

His home, once modest, was clad in marble as his wealth grew. He also owned the Hartman Farms south of Columbus on Route 23, where he kept racehorses and a large herd of dairy cows (the origin of the word "cow town" applied to Columbus). He also built a rustic resort hotel on the farm to bring guests to relax in the "country." Hartman had so much wealth that he constructed the first and only privately owned streetcar line to take guests back and forth from his downtown hotel and the resort hotel on the farm.

But for all the buildings Hartman built, none remains but the Hartman Hotel, now condos, and the many, many pieces of marble that were once part of his home now decorate yards in the Near East Side.

In the mid-1890s, Hartman received the largest order in the company's history from a gentleman in Waco, Texas, and he traveled to Waco with the railcars filled with Pe-Ru-Na to meet the mysterious entrepreneur personally. He brought along his daughter Maribel.

Frederick W. Schumacher, a Danish immigrant who settled in Waco, had placed the large order. Hartman was very impressed by the young man (and his vision of potential sales) and offered him a job in his company to market Pe-Ru-Na. Maribel Hartman was also impressed with the good-

Frederick W. Schumacher, a frequent business associate of Dr. Hartman, had a primary role in the building of the Virginia Apartment Building that was later expanded to include the Virginia Hotel. *Columbus Metropolitan Library Image Collection.*

looking Schumacher. A whirlwind romance culminated in a celebrated wedding in Columbus.

That business and personal partnership proved to be beyond successful for many years. Pe-Ru-Na was sold for $1 a bottle, the equivalent of $65 today. Hartman decided to create a huge advertising budget of $1 million for Schumacher to market Pe-Ru-Na. As vice-president of advertising, Schumacher catapulted Pe-Ru-Na into a worldwide brand. He is widely credited in business history as the "father of modern advertising" for his creation of the testimonial.

The Hartman Hotel's success prompted Schumacher to open his own hotel. He and his father-in-law built the Virginia Apartments (Gay and Third Streets) in 1908, naming it for Schumacher's daughter, who had died as a child. In 1911, it became the Virginia Hotel, and the following year, Hartman transferred full ownership to his son-in-law. (See the Virginia Hotel section.)

In 1914, Schumacher left the business to pursue his own business empire and collect art from galleries across Europe. His marriage to Hartman's daughter was not as lucky as the success of Pe-Ru-Na. Their marriage ended in a very public and bitter divorce shortly before Dr. Hartman passed away. Most of Schumacher's fortune was separated from his wife and Hartman, and husband and wife eventually agreed on terms for their two daughters. Schumacher's fortune remained intact, the Virginia Hotel was his and he had his mansion on East Broad Street.

In addition to all his other accomplishments in advertising and mining, Schumacher was an avid collector of fine art and a supporter of the Columbus Gallery of Fine Arts (now the Columbus Museum of Art), providing funding and resources to build the main building in 1931, and left much of his art collection to the museum. He also founded the Schumacher Gallery at Capital University.

Dr. Hartman's interest in hotels was motivated by different factors. Soon after opening his building in 1898, Dr. Hartman needed additional sleeping rooms for his patients at the nearby Surgical Hotel. Renovated lavish suites were created for wealthy patients. Sky bridges were erected on the second and third floors over Cherry Street, connecting the two buildings and creating what was commonly referred to as the Hartman Sanitarium complex. The term "sanitarium" referred to a medical facility for long-term illness or a health-oriented resort.

In late 1900, Dr. Hartman built a new building for his company headquarters and converted the whole Hartman Sanitarium building into an annex to the surgical hospital. Floor by floor, the building was renovated with the same luxury found in European spas and grand hotels—more hotel than a hospital, with personal valets and lady's maids. The reputation of the Hartman Sanitarium spread, and rooms were

John G. Dunn had a long career as a hotel manager of the second Neil House, the Hartman and the Vendome. In this cartoon, the Vendome is pictured behind him. *Columbus Metropolitan Library Image Collection.*

rented to non-patient guests. Hartman Hotel (also called Hotel Hartman) was created. Hartman and his wife converted a portion of the third floor into a private apartment where he and his family lived in the winter seasons, keeping their mansion five blocks away.

As regular hotel guests quickly started to outnumber patients, the building went from an exclusive hotel for wealthy patients of the surgical hospital to an upgraded grand hotel opened to the general public. Hartman hired the manager of the Neil House, John G. Dunn, to run the hotel. Dunn was a local celebrity in the business, managing other hotels, such as the Vendome Hotel.

The six-story Hotel Hartman was described as the most lavish hotel in Columbus when it opened in November 1902 (much to the disappointment of the owners of the nearby Great Southern Hotel, who quickly upgraded their five-year-old hotel). The Hartman had a restaurant, a French chef and a ballroom. The hotel also advertised an orchestra concert every evening. The *Columbus Dispatch* reported in 1911:

> *The hotel was built as the good Doctor does everything, and as a result it is a more luxuriant and elegantly equipped hotel in Ohio, and ranks well up with any in the United States. An idea as to the way it is equipped is shown by the fact that it contains Oriental rugs the loss of one which would wipe out the profits of the hotel for a month, and that even frames for the outside screen doors are of mahogany.*

The hotel had many features, including a large modern gymnasium, a ladies' parlor, a gentlemen's smoking room, a lavish sixth-floor Gilded Age dining room with hand-painted ceiling murals and the sanitarium baths, which were connected to the main structure by enclosed walking bridges over Cherry Street. The third, fourth and fifth floors contained over one hundred sleeping rooms. Originally, the hotel included a large overhanging porch above the front entrance extending across the five bay-front windows and a veranda on the roof. Around 1905, Hartman expanded his financial empire and opened his own bank, the Market Exchange Bank, removing the hotel gymnasium.

Before 1919, there was no official state-owned residence for the governor's use. Many governors chose their favorite hotels, purchased homes or rented quarters to serve as their residences in the capital city during their terms. In 1906, after being sworn in as governor, Andrew L. Harris chose the Hartman Hotel to serve as his official residence during his term as Ohio's forty-fourth governor (1906–1909). Harris was one of the heroes of the Battle of Gettysburg and the last Civil War general to serve as a state governor in the United States. It is probably a little ironic that Governor Harris's progressive agenda included supporting pure food and drug laws—exactly what brought

This very rare postcard is the only known interior view of the Hartman Hotel.
Private Collection.

An early ad of the Hartman Hotel showing the lavish sixth-floor dining room. *Private Collection.*

down the Hartman empire of alcohol-infused patent medicine. Governor Harris's residence is the only confirmed account of the hotel's use as the official residence of an Ohio governor.

The Hartman Hotel was used by many of the fashionable and famous people of the times. Among them were President Theodore Roosevelt and members of his family. On September 14, 1906, it was as if Lady Gaga, Madonna and Michelle Obama came to town in the person of one woman, Alice Roosevelt Longworth, who arrived in Columbus to dedicate the Statehouse memorial to martyred President McKinley.

"Princess" Alice, the eldest daughter of President Roosevelt, was married to an Ohio congressman from Cincinnati, Nicholas Longworth. In 1906, at age twenty-two, she was as pretty as her cousin Eleanor was plain—as a teenager, she made fun of Eleanor's looks, and as a grown woman, she would enter a room with a cartwheel if she felt she was unnoticed. She was unpredictable.

Her whereabouts were kept secret when she arrived in Columbus. The crowd was estimated to be fifty thousand, but only four thousand had tickets. People mobbed her, and some crawled under the speakers' platform to avoid being crushed. Alice took refuge in the governor's office and then escaped to the Outlook Building (44 East Broad). Eventually, she and her party sought refuge up at the Hartman Hotel, their headquarters, before they left for Cincinnati. She remarked many years later, "Crowds, crowds…Yes, I've seen them all over the world, but I never saw anything that could compare with [that]."

In addition, political activist and author Harriet Taylor Upton, president of the Ohio Women's Suffrage Organization, held organizing meetings in the second-floor parlor of the Hartman Hotel in 1914. In the late 1880s, Susan B. Anthony convinced her to actively join the movement to win the right to vote for women, and Upton rose to leadership roles for the next several decades. She later became the first woman to be vice-chairman of the Republican National Committee in 1920.

In 1961, the *Columbus Dispatch* ran a series of articles in its Sunday magazine over seven weeks titled "The Fabulous Empire of Peruna" about Hartman and his legacy in the city. Columnist Jean Kahler was able to interview many who had worked for Hartman at the Pe-Ru-Na Company, the Hartman Hotel or at his farm. Her collection of articles is one of the most complete insights into Hartman history and covers everything from Hartman's early life to the rise of Pe-Ru-Na as a worldwide bestseller and includes information on the life of Frederick Schumacher, as well as tidbits

The Hartman Hotel restaurant, located on the sixth floor, was one of the most formal dining rooms in Columbus, complete with a French chef and several trained waiters per customer. *Private Collection.*

about the bitter (and very public) Schumacher divorce and Mrs. Hartman's curious demands at the hotel.

Mrs. Hartman immediately called on staff upon arriving at the Hartman suite.

> *"Is Tommy there?" she'd phone to the desk, "Tell him to come up to room 314."*
>
> *Tommy, the employee, knocked on the door.*
> *"Who's there?" she'd say, and open the door, revealing only an eye and a nose.*
> *"Who owns this building?" she would ask.*

"Why, you do," was the reply.
"Then how come everybody's getting better conveniences than I am?
I had to run water out before it got hot. We haven't made our money by
wasting things. When I want hot water I want it right away."

The scenario was repeated daily. Same interrogation, same answers. The employee feared her wrath and recounted that when the telephone rang, he knew he would be the one "in hot water." Water from a two-thousand-gallon tank took time to reach her apartment. Armed with new knowledge from his boss, Tommy eventually confronted her. When she called again, he responded, "Mrs. Hartman, I've already taken it up with Mr. Davis. He's going to fix it up so as soon as you touch it, you'll have hot water. But he needs three figures—we've already got one price of $18,000—"

Mrs. Hartman was stunned, and according to Jean Kahler, that ended the hot water conversations.

Dr. Samuel B. Hartman died at 5:25 p.m. on Wednesday, January 30, 1918, at age eighty-seven in the Hartman Hotel. Some have claimed he died in the elevator going up to the sixth-floor ballroom; however, Kahler reported that Hartman died in bed in his hotel apartments. The family and hotel staff arranged to have his body lay in state in the hotel parlors until the third day after his death, when arrangements could be made with the Congressional Church. The body was taken to Green Lawn Cemetery for private services and, in the spring, was removed from its vault and transported to Lancaster, Pennsylvania, for burial.

An employee of the Hartman Farm, John Morehart, recalled with sadness in 1961, "Pretty near a streetcar load of us went up from the farm to see him before the funeral. They treated us at the hotel as if we all were millionaires. And the old doctor was lying there in the center of it all, looking just as if he was going to tell us one of his big stories."

With Hartman's death and the state government rapidly expanding came the opportunity for more change at the hotel. The idea to construct a new office building first surfaced in 1913, igniting a debate that lasted sixteen years. As the state government continued to grow, the discussion shifted from whether to build a new state-owned building to renting office space. Until a consensus could be reached, state legislators searched for a suitable building to house state offices.

In early May 1921, a little over three years after Dr. Hartman's death, it was announced that the Hartman Hotel would close permanently. A deal had been brokered with the State of Ohio to lease the building and consolidate scattered state departments under one roof. The state was paying an estimated $54,000 per year, with rents set to rise in July 1921 to over $80,000. Ohio Adjutant General Florence had to act quickly on an alternative plan to protect the state budget.

The lease would save the state an estimated $62,000 per year. Acting under authority of an emergency bill passed by both houses of the legislature, Florence closed a deal to lease the building, which was considered the biggest and most satisfactory real estate deal of that time. The Market Exchange Bank on the ground floor would remain, paying the state $5,000 annual rent as reported by the *Columbus Dispatch* in 1921. On May 28, 1921, Governor Harry L. Davis officially signed legislation to lease the hotel. The hotel would close on May 31, 1921, and state possession would begin on July 1, 1921. The law's sponsor, Senator Atwood, announced that very few alterations to the building would be needed.

The Hartman Hotel was known as the Ohio Building, an official state office building. The following state departments were consolidated and moved to the Ohio Building from the Statehouse and the Wyandotte building: the state industrial commission, the state library, the Department of Health, the Department of Highways, the Department of Industrial Relations, the Department of Insurance and Securities and the Commission for the Blind.

The former building provided unexpected perks for state employees. As a cost-saving measure and to speed up the move, no alterations were made to the existing building. Each room, with few exceptions, was in the same configuration as it had been when it was an operating hotel, including private bathrooms. State workers were allowed to come in early to shower, and men could shave before starting their workdays. The first-floor café expanded to a full cafeteria for employees of the building (and opened to the general public) for hot lunches and afternoon coffee breaks. The hotel parlors and main dining room spaces were converted to offices and conference rooms.

The Ohio Building served as the primary center of Ohio state government administration until the Ohio Departments Building (now the Ohio Judicial Center and home to the Ohio Supreme Court) was opened in 1933. The Ohio Building continued to house various state offices throughout the next several decades. The Market Exchange Bank remained on the ground floor (run by the Hartman family trust) and was open for the banking needs of Columbus residents and state employees who worked above.

In the early 1960s, Huntington National Bank acquired the Market Exchange Bank and purchased the building from the Hartman trust. For the next twenty years, the bank remained, and the floors above were filled with various tenants, ranging from offices of lawyers and private detectives to furniture, clothing and jewelry stores. The Ohio Bureau of Motor Vehicles was the last of the state departments to remain in the building until the early 1970s.

With the demolition of the Hartman building in 1981 (an office building attached to the Hartman Theater at State and Third Streets), the former Hartman Hotel was the last tangible reminder of the Hartman empire in downtown. In 1992, the bank branch of Huntington and the rest of the building closed, and for the next several years, the building remained vacant and fell into disrepair.

In mid-1999, Larry Rubin of Plaza Properties and three other partners purchased the building and began a multimillion-dollar renovation for street-level retail and office space on the five remaining floors. During the inspection of the building, the original hand-painted murals in the sixth-floor ballroom were discovered. A drop ceiling had hidden them for many years and rendered unknown to the people who worked in the space for decades. Plans were adapted to use the second floor and the sixth-floor ballroom as event spaces.

The restoration refurbished the exterior and added windows to the rear of the building where buildings once stood. A modern glass staircase was added to the rear of the building where the original fire escape stairs were located. Designed by Columbus architect Jonathan Barnes, the glass structure received the Award of Merit from the American Institute of Architects in 2002. The original sixth-floor ballroom also received an extensive renovation, led by Sullivan and Bruck Architects, to become a popular wedding and event destination.

The building saw changes between 2005 and 2008 with residential conversions of floors two through six into the Hartman Loft Condominiums, now home to over sixty downtown residents. Even though the lavish ballroom on the sixth floor was restored in 2001 (at a cost of around $200,000), out of financial necessity, the developer gutted the ballroom space and converted it into residential condos. However, as of 2015, there are still many original elements remaining throughout the building, including mosaic tile floors and decorative tin and mahogany ceilings. The Hartman Hotel building and the Westin Great Southern Hotel are the only hotel buildings still standing in Columbus of the five Gilded Age grand hotels.

THE DESHLER-WALLICK HOTEL

The Pen and Pencil Club of Columbus, a newspaper clipping book, described the Deshler Hotel in 1915, reflecting the excitement and publicity of a building that would not open until August 23, 1916:

> *This hotel will contain four hundred rooms of which three hundred and fifty will have private baths and the balance will have running water. It will be twelve stories in height. The two lower floors will be done in gray Terra Cotta, above which will be eight stories of Greendale "Rug" Brick in autumnal shades, the remaining two floors being a combination of the brick and Terra Cotta. There will be window boxes for flowers in the large restaurant windows on the first*

This photo shows a portion of the exterior cornice detail on the stone façade of the Deshler Hotel. *Columbus Metropolitan Library Image Collection.*

The Deshler Hotel Ladies' Parlor. Elaborate appointments such as these drove construction costs above $1.5 million. *Columbus Metropolitan Library Image Collection.*

floor and entirely around the house on the third and eleventh floors. This gives a floral effect on the outside of the building about seven hundred feet in length.

The lobby and all the principal rooms will have artificial ventilation—all the air in them being washed and changed every few

*moments and cooled in summer. The feature of the hotel will be a large
ball-room, located on the second floor that can be used for conventions and
meetings of all descriptions. This room is ninety feet square with a gallery
entirely surrounding it, and will easily seat a thousand people. Adjoining
the ball-room will be a service kitchen which will be able to serve 500
people. The grill room will be located in the basement and men's café in
addition to the regular restaurant on the first floor. The private dining rooms
are located on the second floor, adjoining the ball-room. This whole floor
can be used for entertainment purposes when desired.*

David Deshler and his wife, Betsy Greene Deshler, came to Columbus
in 1817 as new homesteaders in Ohio from Easton, Pennsylvania. For the
unheard-of sum of $1,000 and a gold pocket watch, they bought what
would become the most prominent lot in Columbus, the northwest corner of
Broad and High Streets. It would remain in the Deshler family for over 150
years. Betsy died ten weeks after giving birth to their second son, William.
David remarried and had a number of daughters. William and his son,
John, became partners in a number of endeavors—including the Hocking
Valley Railroad, the Ohio Natural Gas and Fuel Company, Buckeye Steel
Castings Company and Columbus's first skyscraper across from the Deshler
homestead, the Wyandotte Building, designed by Chicago's Daniel Burnham.

In the late 1870s, David's son William removed his parents' modest home
and replaced it with the Deshler Block, which consisted of the retail space and
offices. David Deshler's grandson John planned a hotel based on family stories
of his grandfather's dream for the corner. He selected a well-known firm of
Chicago architects who had previously built the Tacoma Building in Chicago
in 1889. That building became a model for steel-framed high-rise buildings.
William died six months before the opening of the hotel. There were earlier
plans that called for a much larger hotel, but they were never realized.

Over time, owners and names changed. The hotel was called the Deshler-
Wallick, the Deshler Hilton, the Deshler-Cole and the Deshler-Beasley. Cole
took over after a dispute with Hilton, but the glory years were clearly under
the management of Wallick.

William Deshler influenced the landscape of East Broad Street after a visit
to Havana, Cuba. Impressed with the wide streets and boulevards, Deshler
persuaded the city to create tree-lined planting strips and carriage lanes on
Broad Street. They were done in, decades later, by car pollution and the
perceived need for more traffic lanes; however, every few years there is an
attempt to revisit the idea and re-create the Deshler dream.

Right: John Deshler was the son of William Deshler and grandson of David Deshler who fulfilled his family's dream of building a hotel on the corner of Broad and High. Note the blackface caricatures that represent the racial views of the early twentieth century. *Columbus Metropolitan Library Image Collection.*

Below: The front desk lobby of the Deshler Wallick Hotel at Christmastime in the late 1940s. *Grandview Heights Public Library.*

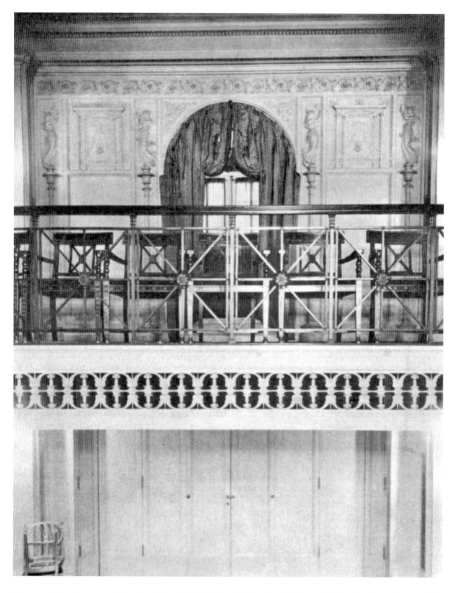

The main ballroom of the Deshler-Wallick Hotel. In the 1930s and '40s, the hotel hosted all of the big bands. *Columbus Metropolitan Library Image Collection.*

When the hotel opened in 1916, five hundred guests were treated to what was called the largest social event of the year in a building that was described as Pompeiian style by the *American Antiquities Journal*. Many came from out of town by the trainloads. The Wallicks were in charge, and their reputations preceded them because of their hotels in New York and Cleveland.

Gold table service; luxury furnishings costing $400,000; hand-decorated bedroom suites; a telephone switchboard that could serve a town of five thousand and a gigantic Oriental rug that cost $15,000 (and was later replaced by an even larger one in 1936 that cost $35,000) were only a few of

Telephone operators at the Deshler-Wallick Hotel with supervisor Ada Kurtzman looking on in 1948. *Grandview Heights Public Library.*

its luxuries. That rug was said to be the largest ever imported to the United States. The carpet took two years and one hundred Persian workers to create. The Eastern set of guests presented the hotel with a copper Russian coffee service estimated to cost $1,500.

Two days later, the hotel was thrown open for public viewing—and the women of Columbus lined the street by the thousands for a chance to visit the famed hotel. Three hundred employees waited for them. Most of the employees had been brought to Columbus from New York.

There were tea dances every afternoon, a splendid Ionian Room for both men and women and a separate restaurant for men only. The orchestras changed frequently, with jazz combos brought in from New York and Marimba bands from "Gautemalia." The hotel hosted New Year's Eve parties, the Crystal Room diners, five chamber music concerts and the return of Parker's Popular Players on a regular basis. More people were introduced to jazz at the Deshler-Wallick than anywhere else in Columbus, except perhaps on Mt. Vernon Avenue.

The Madrid Cocktail Lounge, located in the Deshler-Hilton Hotel, pictured in 1954. *Grandview Heights Public Library.*

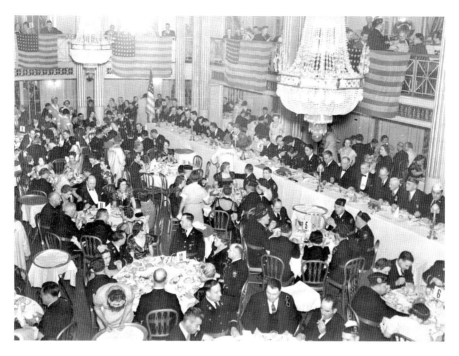

The main banquet room at the Deshler-Wallick Hotel in the late 1930s. *Grandview Heights Public Library.*

It took forty bartenders to serve the customers at the huge bar. French chefs and restaurateurs who had worked at the Plaza and the Knickerbocker Hotels in New York prepared the dinners. Guests were not permitted in the dining rooms unless they were in semiformal dress in the afternoons and formal dress in the evenings. The headwaiter and others wore Prince Albert coats.

Frequent dining visitors were Warren G. Harding, Henry Ford, Claude Meeker (a famous and wealthy stockbroker) and W.H. Button (a breeder of Belgian horses). When Meeker's daughter was married at the Deshler, the gold service was brought out. Kept under tight security, it was perhaps used only ten times in the history of the hotel.

Dayton millionaire Governor James Cox honeymooned there and then stayed to reside in the hotel. His Chicago socialite bride changed only the color of the drapes.

"The horsey set" loved the Deshler and its furnishings—the name referring to the class of people who could afford polo ponies, racehorses and competition show horses. The Beaux Arts Ball and the Matrix dinner celebrants and the Kit Kat Club were catered to at the hotel.

Later, manager Charles "Curly" Cole attempted to enliven the hotel with a bit of sensation while guests ate dinner or sipped drinks. He created what he called the Roaring Twenties in the dining room. A pretty young girl in tights ascended a ladder to a swing suspended from the ceiling, swaying back and forth to the orchestra music. Some older patrons were shocked. He also created a ten- by eight-foot bed in his private suite, room 1212, and placed "an art work" on the sidewall that was activated by a switch. The artwork produced thunder and lightning.

The hotel owners seemed to have their eccentric moments. Fred Beasley, a millionaire who knew nothing about the hotel business, once road his horse into the lobby and into an elevator, asking to be taken to his room.

Even from its early years, the Deshler had its share of scandals. In 1917, the body of Mona Byron Simon was found in a luxurious room with bullets through her heart. A sensational murder was not what the hotel wanted, and her body was quickly removed at midnight through a back door. The coroner "forgot" to tell the press. Hers was not the only covered-up murder.

In 1927, an expansion of the Deshler-Wallick Hotel—including a connector to the new rooms in the American Insurance Union (AIU) Citadel, called the Venetian Bridge—was celebrated by the arrival of the flamboyant New York mayor Jimmie Walker, who vowed he would take a sip of champagne in every room. He was known as a heavy drinker, but with six hundred new rooms, he could not make good on his promise.

Louis Wallick had been good for the hotel even before 1927, when he convinced John Deshler to build his father and grandfather's dream. In the years before the crash of the stock market, Wallick's personal magnetism influenced John Lentz, builder of the AIU, and owners of the Biltmore Hotels, but his heart was in the Columbus hotel. Like most hotels during the Depression, the Deshler-Wallick was only half full, but Wallick managed to meet expenses. After World War II, he made a dramatic comeback, and the Deshler was literally in full swing with the Ionian Room, big bands and the loyal customers of the rich set who were anxious to put World War II behind them.

During this reopening, full-page newspaper spreads covered every aspect of the upgrades and changes—tiled baths, stronger safes, the new leases for the AIU Citadel, the laundry service, the new $1 million furnishings, lounging rooms for artists, the radio station WAIU, twenty miles of plumbing pipe and more. Every company in Columbus seems to have had a contract for the remodeling.

Now officially named the Deshler-Wallick Hotel, the Deshler roared in the 1920s—especially when Ohio State football, reaching a frenzy, was fueled by illegal booze. Furniture was thrown out the windows.

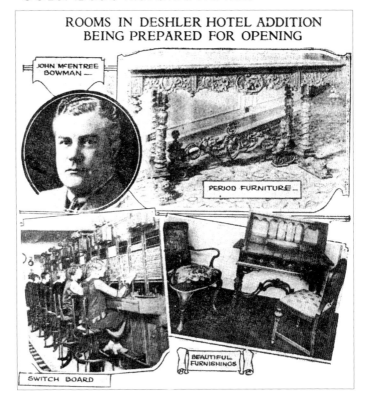

ROOMS IN DESHLER HOTEL ADDITION
BEING PREPARED FOR OPENING

JOHN McENTREE BOWMAN —

PERIOD FURNITURE —

BEAUTIFUL FURNISHINGS

SWITCH BOARD

The Deshler was known for its artwork and elaborate furnishings. *Columbus Metropolitan Library Image Collection.*

The Sky Room in the Deshler-Hilton, with a view from the sixteenth floor overlooking the Scioto River, was a popular place for dinners and dancing. *Columbus Metropolitan Library Image Collection.*

Luggage labels were popular souvenirs that helped to advertise where guests had stayed. This is a Deshler label from the 1930s. *Private Collection.*

Still others chose to take life more quietly and live there as permanent residents—Mrs. Robert Wolfe, in her widowhood; Mrs. Battelle and her son, the owner of the Sells Floto Circus; Carl Hoster the brewer; and industrialists and coal magnates.

The Deshler had its share of famous guests, and because it was on the most prominent corner of the city, it was often the backdrop for photos of celebrations—like the regiments that marched off to World War I and World War II and, hopefully, marched home again.

The front door of the Deshler was the scene of Victory Bond sales in World War I and the political theater of anti-German sentiments against the kaiser. In a city made up mostly of those with German descent, the sentiments were more to reaffirm American politics.

There were also guests who wanted to stay under the radar. On July 7, 1953, former president Harry Truman and his wife, Bess, drove into town on their way back to Missouri. They drove their own car and had no bodyguards and no reservations. They rolled up about noon to the front door and entered the lobby. At first they were not noticed, but when President Truman asked for a room, heads turned.

A dozen squealing teenage girls from a Future Homemakers of American convention ran to greet them. Historian Matthew Alego described the finer details: "The unexpected appearance of the former president and first lady at their [hotel]…practically sent the girls into delirium. They nearly tore the hotel drug store apart in their rush to purchase film for their cameras." The

On the corner of Broad and High, a parade of the Thirty-seventh Division with the newly completed Deshler-Wallick in the background. Notice the sign of the Mills Restaurant north of the hotel. *Columbus Metropolitan Library Image Collection.*

A scene in the Deshler-Wallick Hotel during President Truman's visit in March 1946. The president is at the microphone with Bishop G. Bromley Oxnam. President Truman would return to the Deshler both as president and as former president. *Grandview Heights Public Library.*

Trumans were given room 1663, ordering room service for lunch. Alego continued in his book, *Harry Truman's Excellent Adventure*, "After lunch, Harry took a nap while America's future homemakers stalked the corridors of the Deshler in search of him."

Bess went to the hotel beauty shop, reported the *Columbus Dispatch*, which also stalked the couple. She "emerged looking rested and stylish with small curls covering her head and fluffy bangs topped her forehead." The Trumans ordered in dinner, checking out the next morning at 9:00 a.m., waving goodbye and heading for home.

In the 1940s, the Deshler had another guest (although his presence was kept low profile). Senator Joe McCarthy, the Cold War warrior who led the charge against suspected Communists, stayed at the Deshler. Prior to his fame of blacklisting writers and actors in Hollywood, he was frequently in Columbus as part of his job with postwar housing funding. While at the Deshler, he ordered ahead for some of his favorite pastimes—good liquor, poker buddies and prostitutes.

In 1947, Chicago developer Julius Epstein bought control of the hotel interests in what some called "a cash deal" that reportedly involved $2 million. In 1950, there was trouble between the Deshler interests and 50 West Broad, the

Exterior street view of the Deshler-Wallick in the early 1960s, when the corner of Broad and High was still the center of Columbus. *Columbus Metropolitan Library Image Collection.*

operators of the LeVeque Tower (former AIU Citadel), and in an out-of-court settlement, 50 West Broad took over the hotel's interests held by the Chicago owners. In 1953, the hotel changed names to the Deshler-Hilton. The Deshler-Hilton began remodeling the grand ballroom, redid hotel rooms with all new furniture and drapes, began to put in air conditioning and spent over $2 million on a complete face-lift for the hotel. Hilton interests brought in Charles (Curly) Cole, and the name changed again to Deshler-Cole the following year.

As the Deshler-Cole, the hotel gave up the rights to the six hundred rooms in the LeVeque, accessible by the Venetian Bridge. The lovely terra cotta arched bridge was removed in November 1964, and the Deshler-Cole

A 1968 photo shows the twelve-story brick and stone Deshler-Beasley Hotel on the corner of High and Broad Streets. The photo was shot from an elevated position from across the street at the Statehouse. *Grandview Heights Public Library.*

worked to restore its own four hundred rooms. Old partitions gave way to suites, new carpets and drapes were purchased and an antenna system was installed to connect new television receivers (that allowed three channels, the OSU education station and three radio stations to be accessible in every room). Vending machines, false ceilings, rooms with four double beds and remote control television to check in on the conference rooms were "perks" of what was now being called "a luxury hotel."

With added costs for static revenue, the Deshler-Cole went into receivership on June 6, 1966 (an oddly prophetic combination of disastrous numbers). A receiver was appointed for William Cox, trustee of the Deshler trust. By the following month, the hotel had been officially sold to Fred Beasley, a Columbus and Athens auto dealer, who renamed it the Deshler-Beasley. Again, there was talk of big plans for renovations. The newspapers and the pundits all pointed to the hotel's failures as the failures of Cole's policies. The separation from the AIU was deemed a disaster.

The lavishly decorated first-story exterior of the Deshler Hotel. Over the years, the grand hotel was known by various names such as the Deshler-Hilton and the Deshler-Cole. *Columbus Metropolitan Library Image Collection.*

The loss of six hundred rooms—and even more when he combined rooms to make suites—was terrible. Cole was unable to meet his $7,000 a week employee payroll. The troubles of the Deshler were not isolated incidents but part of the larger economic picture of the country. Perhaps there was more discretionary income for an individual in the post–World War II boom, but the forecast for downtown and downtown hotels was still too far on the horizon to be seen as a storm warning. All hotels pinned their hopes on the return of big conventions.

In 1967, the *Columbus Dispatch*'s headline read, "Court Decision Could Pave Way for Landmark Sale, 'Exciting Things'—TROUBLE

WEIGHS, BUT THERE MAY ALWAYS BE A 'DESHLER.'" The real problem—unpaid water bills aside—was a trust that said the property could not be sold. Everyone said there were plenty of buyers; if only the property was available, exciting things could happen again.

The hotel business went to a new firm: Capital Trading Company. But despite all of the transfers and transactions, the hotel remained in the hands of the Deshler trust set up in 1898. The trust had stipulated that it could not be terminated until twenty-one years after the death of William Deshler's five children. Helen Deshler Brown of New York City was still living when an heir of the Deshler estate, Frederick Stanton III of Columbus, filed suit in Franklin County Common Pleas Court to have the trust terminated.

On May 23, 1968, Judge Leonard Stern ordered the trust terminated and the property sold because, on behalf of John Stanton III, grandson of William Deshler, the real estate was not providing sufficient income for beneficiaries of the trust he had set up. In fact, not only was there insufficient income for the heirs, but the property was also seriously delinquent, the city sewer and water bills were unpaid and there were liens on the property.

It was widely speculated that local financier John Galbreath was interested in the site and would save the Deshler. Within a day of the judge's decision, resident businesses and offices said they would stay through July—Delta Airlines, United Airlines, the Busy Bee Restaurant, Perkins Pancake House, Gray Drugstore, Union News Company, Rockefeller for President Headquarters, Your Gift Shop, Cosmetique of Columbus, DeSantis barbershop, Central Ticket Office and Ross Ree's Men's Clothing—while looking for a downtown space.

The Deshler closed its doors on July 31, 1968. Fond memories flooded out to the newspapers. There were stories about Tommy Dorsey's band, the banquet for General John "Black Jack" Pershing, the late visit to the bar by Clarence Darrow after he debated Rabbi Tarshish in Memorial Hall, the banquet for Ohio State legend Chic Harley, the never verified appearance of Al Capone, the Maramor Candy Shop and the Newark, Ohio Klan members accused of abducting a manicurist. Others in Columbus most likely waited for the announcement of the auction where they could buy a sterling silver tea set with "Deshler" engraved on it—just to make the memory last a little longer.

On September 24, 1969, protective barricades went up around the Deshler to begin demolition. The American International had planned to build a fifty-seven-story hotel and office complex, but a 2,200-space parking garage west of Veteran's Memorial and a transportation system were to be completed first. Nothing was ever built. Years later, One Columbus—the office building on the hotel's former site—was constructed.

4

ELEGANT, AFFORDABLE AND CONVENIENT ACCOMMODATIONS

In addition to the five grande dame hotels, there were other hotels that had elegance and style but were still affordable and accessible. These hotels generally catered to businessmen, as well as provided more affordable long-term housing for legislators, single or elderly residents or individuals who wanted the conveniences of a full-service hotel. These hotel residents were in most cases allowed to decorate their rooms as they saw fit, including hanging artwork. As hotel residents, they were afforded all the amenities the hotel had to offer for regular guests: room service, turndown service, laundry service and daily housekeeping. In the case of elderly residents, it was common for hotel staff to regularly check in on guests and report any concerns to their doctors.

THE VIRGINIA HOTEL

The Virginia Hotel was part hotel and part full-service apartment building constructed by Frederick W. Schumacher and his father-in-law, Dr. Samuel B. Hartman. In late 1912, Schumacher became the sole owner until his death in the late 1950s. The hotel was constructed on the site of the Central Christian Church and the Zettler Grocery.

When announced in 1906, the building was intended to be a "modern bachelors' hall" for men only with fifty-five apartments suites consisting

The exterior of the Virginia Hotel resembled the Seneca, which followed later. Both were designed by Frank Packard. *Private Collection.*

of a sitting room, bedroom and bathroom. The original architect was Mr. Hurdenberg of New York City; however, Schumacher was unimpressed with his designs and turned to Frank Packard for the final design, which left room to build new wings in the future if the project was successful (which it turned out to be).

As construction began, the demand and interest increased, and Schumacher and Hartman modified the plans to designate a portion for families. It was completed in 1908. The ground floor contained several shops and a large café "for the convenience of the tenants in the building."

The apartments on the first floor had multiple bedrooms and were designed exclusively for families. The upper floors were reserved for bachelors. Options included having fully furnished or partially furnished rooms. When the building opened, the apartments were described as elegant rooms with artistic furniture, telephones and baths. Bachelors filled them quickly. Although it was originally solely an apartment building, it had all the amenities of a hotel, including telephones in each room connected to the front desk where "clerks and bellboys will be constantly on duty to respond to the wants of the occupants." The building was expanded in 1911, and a new wing included the hotel. Among its eateries were the Jefferson Room, the Grotto Room and the Virginia Hotel Coffee Shop.

ELEGANT, AFFORDABLE AND CONVENIENT ACCOMMODATIONS

The lobby of the Virginia Hotel, designed by Frank Packard, was open an airy and resembled the Great Southern Hotel's lobby, designed by Yost and Packard. *Private Collection.*

For years, the Virginia Hotel was a "neutral zone" meeting place for newspaper reporters from rival papers. The location was conveniently north of both the *Columbus-Citizen Journal* and the *Columbus Dispatch* and east of the *Ohio State Journal*. The hotel was the perfect place for all three newspaper staffs to meet for a cocktail at the bar or card games in the hotel basement, discussing the latest political gossip (or triumph to recruit the competition to their own newspaper). It was in the hotel bar that the Columbus Press Club was born. Although the Neil House would serve as the epicenter for politicos to hold court with bourbon, the Press Club was usually for people in the newspaper business. After a few years, the club relocated from the Virginia to the Deshler-Wallick and AIU and then to its own quarters on the second floor of the Franklin Printing Company.

In the 1940s, the hotel's newspaper advertisements declared, "Hotel Virginia: Luxurious Simplicity" and "A Safe Place for Your Family to Stop."

Reverend Father William Dunn and his sister, Sister Ellen Dunn, lived in the Virginia Hotel Apartments from 1943 to 1947 and shared their memories with Ann Seren, a member of the Columbus Landmarks Foundation's education committee. The Dunn family was associated with downtown hotels from late nineteenth and early twentieth centuries. John G. Dunn managed the second Neil House, the Hartman Hotel and the Vendome Hotel, among others, during his career.

Father Dunn recalled his childhood and Columbus life around the hotel in the 1940s:

> *We lived in the Virginia Hotel, Third and E. Gay Sts. Our father, William A. Dunn was the manager. We attended St. Joseph Cathedral for church and the St. Joseph Cathedral School. The school was the "old Kelly mansion," situated on E. Broad St. where Sixth St. meets Broad. One of the hotel bellboys, Frank Cruise, was assigned to walk us to school.*
>
> *Mother would take us along this route to the Columbus Public Library on Grant Ave. Occasionally we sat on benches or played on the library lawn. Robert Stevenson, head librarian, lived at the Virginia Hotel. He was a bachelor who went each year by train to take in the plays in New York. He would give me his copy of* The New Yorker *when I was a teenager. That started me on becoming a lifelong reader and subscriber.*
>
> *East of the hotel, on Gay St. were several commercial buildings. Across Fourth St. was the Masonic Temple, at the corner of Gay & Fourth, then a barber shop and next to it, a Chinese laundry, operated by the Yee family. The Cathedral priests patronized the barber shop. The Yee children*

The Virginia Hotel ballroom was a popular event space for newspapermen and conventions. *Private Collection.*

*attended Cathedral school with us. They lived above the laundry and we
visited them several times.*

*The Virginia faced Third St. Exiting its front door, one passed several
shops renting street level space in the hotel; a haberdasher and one or two
others. The last door, as one walked south, was the entrance to the hotel
cocktail lounge. An alley, more like a walkway, separated the hotel from
the* Citizen-Journal *newspaper building. Newspaper staff, including
the men who ran the presses, frequently patronized the hotel bar. The
pressmen wore caps fashioned out of newspaper pages, sort of square and
close-fitting to their heads. Trucks would deliver huge rolls of paper that
were rolled off the bed of the truck and lowered by sidewalk elevator to
the basement presses. We watched these deliveries with fascination.*

Catter-corner across Third St. from the Citizen *was a diner, named
Tom Thumbs, where there was a counter with stools. Office workers
patronized it, and if the dining room in the hotel was closed, guests
would send the bellboys over to the diner to buy carry-out dinner to eat
in their guest room.*

Sister Ellen added:

*My family resided in Suite 317 with my mother Marion Tehan Dunn, and
my two brothers: William and John. I was three to seven years old during
these years.*

*We had a real field day in those years, playing in the Hotel and
in the downtown area. We had a roof play yard (we went out a hall
window) which overlooked the newspaper,* Citizen-Journal, *and
we would wave at employees, watch them off-load those huge rolls of
paper, etc. They once took a picture of us playing in our "outdoor"
space and printed it on the front page of* Citizen-Journal—*without
my parents' permission!*

*On Sunday evenings, we would walk up Gay St. to High St. and eat
at Marzetti's or go to the Southern Hotel when the dining room at the
Virginia was closed. That was always an adventure!*

In the early 1960s, after the hotel was razed and the new Sheraton-
Columbus Hotel (now the Renaissance Hotel) was built on the site, a plaque
was placed dedicating the Virginia Room by Captain H. Mowery, who
served as executive vice-president of the Ohio Hotel & Motel Association
for over fifty years. The plaque read:

Preserving A Memory

This N. Third & Gay St. corner now the address of The Sheraton Columbus Hotel was the site for nearly seven decades of *HOTEL VIRGINIA* created, owned and operated by *FREDERICK W. SCHUMACHER* Prominent Columbus Investor who gave generously of his earned wealth to the Columbus Gallery of Fine Arts now the Columbus Museum of Art. Many of his donated works are still on view at the museum.

After Mr. Schumacher built the hotel he named it *HOTEL VIRGINIA* in honor of his wife. We deemed it appropriate to preserve the valued Columbus memory by naming this *THE VIRGINIA ROOM.*

Ohio Supreme Court Justices and members of the Ohio General Assembly lived at the Virginia while they were in Columbus for official duties returning home on weekends. Mr. Schumacher enjoyed relating he had convinced the Ohio Republican Party to have its 1916 convention and its pre-Presidential rally in Columbus and The Virginia Hotel was designated as headquarters for the historic event.

However, Mr. Schumacher was prouder to relate he had a major part in convincing the G.A.R. (Grand Army of the Republic) and its Auxiliary, The W.R.C. (Women's Relief Corps) to hold its national convention in Columbus in 1924 and to designate The Virginia Hotel as headquarters for the officers of the G.A.R. and the W.R.C. Civil War veterans and their benevolent wives, daughters and sisters formed their traditional Fife and Drum Corps parade in front of the beautifully landscaped and palatial Schumacher home at E. Broad St. and Hamilton Park and marched proudly west on Broad St. to the State Capitol where the Governor of Ohio saluted their flags as they marched to the music of their bands.

This plaque is designated to
inspire our most pleasant moments—those filled
with Memories

There was an error in the plaque text. Schumacher did not name the hotel after his wife. This is a common mistake made repeatedly since 1911. It is possible Schumacher never corrected anyone because he did not want to speak of his ex-wife and their bitter divorce or the sorrow caused by the death of his daughter, for whom the hotel is actually named.

After years of remodeling and various owners, the plaque and the room name no longer exist.

THE SENECA HOTEL

Did you know that Columbus was the temporary home of a famous Cuban family? In 1959, shortly after toppling the Cuban regime of President Fulgencio Batista, Fidel Castro, out of an abundance of caution and fear of their safety, quietly moved his mother and sister into the Seneca Hotel.

For years, this story was an urban legend in Columbus until the late Mike Hardin, popular columnist of the *Columbus Dispatch*, tracked down Beatrice Rhodebeck in July 2001. Rhodebreck, known as Miss Bea, started working at the Seneca in 1949, spending the next quarter century at the hotel front desk. She ran the hotel in every regard, "save title and salary."

"When Fidel took over," Rhodebeck told Hardin, "his sister and mother came to the Seneca in May and left in September. She [Castro's mother] always wore a complete black outfit; black veil, shawl, gloves. They went to Mass every morning."

Fidel Castro's brother and current president of Cuba, Raoul Castro, came to Columbus to collect his mother and sister and was shocked to learn how much they had enjoyed themselves in Columbus. Rhodebeck observed of Castro's sister, "She was spending money like water. When Raoul came to pick them up and saw the bill, he about had a heart attack. He jumped all over me, and I jumped right back."

After Raoul had whisked his kin to Port Columbus, Rhodebeck said, he telephoned her from the airport still hot from their disagreement. "He said, 'I have never had a woman talk to me like that, and one of these days I'm going to come back and take care of you.'" She told Hardin she was always mystified by why the Castro women chose Columbus, and Hardin speculated that as a remote hideout, Columbus certainly possessed distinct advantage over Miami.

Seneca Hotel
COLUMBUS, OHIO
HALF BLOCK EAST OF MEMORIAL HALL

LOBBY VIEW

The Seneca Hotel was designed by noted architect Frank Packard. *Private Collection.*

Built in 1917, the Seneca Hotel was designed by renowned Columbus architect Frank Packard and is listed on the National Register of Historic Places. The structure is made up of a ten-story tower, a four-story building and a smaller two-story component.

Packard was America's foremost institutional architect, designing over 3,400 buildings, including over 100 business and residential buildings in Columbus alone. Buildings designed by Packard in the Columbus area include: Columbus Savings and Trust (Atlas Building), the YMCA, the Huntington Bank Building, Capitol Trust (8 on the Square), the Masonic Temple (Columbus Atheneum), the Lindenberg Mansion (the first official governor's mansion, now home of the Columbus Foundation), the T&O Railroad Station, North High School, Orton Hall, the Sells Circus House and many other hotels.

Packard had the Seneca Indian tribe in mind when he designed the building with Indian heads adorning the front and Seneca Indian symbols and images engraved on each doorknob. The Seneca Hotel—with well-appointed suites, large ballrooms and a rooftop garden—became a popular location for Columbus socialites and visitors.

The hotel advertised "220 rooms and suites, circulating ice water in every room, two dining rooms—exceptional but not expensive, two unique beverage rooms with a lobby entrance to our own fireproof garage." It was listed as both "residential" and "transient." The building served primarily as a hotel but also housed long-term apartments. Advertised as the Seneca Plaza at State and Grant Streets, it consisted of 100 apartments and 120 suites and offices under the same management. Other parts of the building housed retail and office spaces, credit unions, lawyers' offices and the University Club, which later relocated to the top of the American Education Press building across from the Statehouse.

Mike Hardin's interview with Beatrice Rhodebeck provided more than just the Castro story. She said that the hotel once provided a safe haven for a Cleveland union official, winged by gunfire during a power struggle. He sought a temporary refuge in the hotel and came with an armed guard outside the room.

In addition to the families of dictators and wounded union bosses, the Seneca was also the hideout for the Ohio State football team before a big home game during Woody Hayes's reign. The coach paced the hallways like an army general preparing for an invasion to enforce a strict curfew and demanded that the telephone switchboard block all incoming calls from the players' female friends.

"Woody never went to bed," Rhodebeck said of those nights. "He'd sit up all night, go up and down the halls, come down to the lobby and read the newspaper."

The Seneca Hotel was the home of the University Club before it moved to Third Street. *Private Collection.*

In the late 1960s and early '70s, the hotel business began to decline, and the hotel was showing its age. The hotel's longtime owner, James Michos, was forced to sell the building because he could no longer afford to keep it up to his standards. "He came to me with tears running down his face," Rhodebeck remembered. When Rhodebeck first started, it was a different era, the age of "jeweled dowagers" of the Downtown hotel business (Seneca, Southern, Deshler and the Neil House) that oozed "an urbane refinement, a sense of propriety that bordered on the pretentious," said Mike Hardin.

Rhodebeck fondly recalled Michos: "On a Saturday night, he would come down to the lobby in tails. He mingled among the cocktail crowd, inquiring about service and accommodations in the manner of a solicitous cruise-ship captain."

Beatrice Rhodebeck left soon after Michos did. The hotel changed owners and tried to remain open. In 1967, most of the apartments were vacated or turned into rooms for students attending the Nationwide Beauty Academy. The building went through several tenants, including the Columbus Teachers Credit Union. The State of Ohio took up residency in 1973 in a large part of the building for the next fifteen years, housing the Ohio Environmental Protection Agency.

After the exodus of state offices in 1987, the building was abandoned and fell into disrepair. But the drama the hotel saw in the past was replaced with a different type of drama—this time from developers, potential buyers, zoning officials, preservationists and building inspectors. In 1991, a Cincinnati company made a bid to buy the building to tear it down for a parking lot, and attorney Robert Shamansky, with the backing of preservationists, bought the building for $300,000 with a plan to convert it into apartments. Zoning and parking issues arose for the next five years and prevented the plan from becoming a reality. City building inspectors asked to have the building declared a public nuisance after exterior damage went unrepaired. In 1996, Shamansky abandoned his plans for an apartment building based on zoning issues that allowed for little to no parking if the building was converted. Frequent requested permits for demolition were denied.

The building's future was uncertain until the Casto company purchased the building with a new plan for redevelopment. This plan would prove to be unsuccessful. However, all of the nine lives of the Seneca were not spent. With a new location of the Capital Law School and the growth of Columbus College of Art and Design nearby, Campus Apartments bought the Seneca in 2004 with a viable plan that had a nearby potential market and solutions to previous zoning issues; this time, the Seneca would see a plan come to fruition.

In 2008, the Seneca Hotel opened its doors after twenty years of vacancy and several years of extensive renovation. It was restored at last. The building now houses over one hundred apartments and retail space on the ground level. It is a central part of the Discovery District.

The Fort Hayes Hotel

Construction began on the Fort Hayes Hotel (33 West Spring Street) in early 1923 and was completed over a year later. It opened on November 11, 1924, with C.C. Schiffler as managing director. The building was constructed out of concrete in a Chicago School architectural style and was 168 feet tall with fourteen floors, three hundred rooms and eight banquet rooms, including the Crystal Room. Like the Seneca Hotel, the Fort Hayes was a moderately priced hotel. It was within three blocks of Union Station and in proximity to the heart of downtown, as well as to shopping and theaters.

When it opened, rates were $3.50 and up, far more affordable than other downtown hotels like the nearby Deshler. Each room was advertised as being an outside-facing room with a private bath. The Fort Hayes was a popular place for meetings and conventions for many years and was regarded as a very affordable and comfortable alternative for out-of-town guests and for banquets.

Announcing the formal opening on November 24, 1924, Schiffler took out a very large advertisement in the *Columbus Citizen* cordially inviting the people of Columbus and Central Ohio to attend the formal opening gala of the hotel: "Visitors will find that Columbus' newest and most up-to-date hotel has been built with a regard for beauty as well as comfort. In the lobbies may be seen the $100,000 collection of antique furniture from the estate of the late Sarah Bernhardt. On the walls will be found many masterpieces, the work of famous artists."

The Bernhardt collection was remembered decades later, but so were the restaurants—the English Grill, the Ritz Room and the ballroom. With $100,000 worth of antiques and artwork from Bernhardt in the lobby and dining rooms and with the executive suites of walnut and mahogany, the other furnishings had to be impressive, too. The sleeping rooms were modest compared to the high standards of the Deshler, Neil and Southern Hotels.

The Fort Hayes Hotel had fourteen floors and was home to the celebrated Crystal Room restaurant. *Private Collection.*

ELEGANT, AFFORDABLE AND
CONVENIENT ACCOMMODATIONS

By 1930, only a few years after opening, the hotel was in serious trouble and in receivership. Only a few pieces of the Sarah Bernhardt collection remained, and there was shock at the incredible deterioration of the six-year-old hotel.

However, help was on the way. The Crystal Room restaurant made the Fort Hayes famous for many years to come. After the Albert Pick Company bought the hotel in the early 1930s, it brought in Robert I. Griffith as managing director to bring the hotel back to life. Under Griffith's direction, the Crystal Room, the hotel's main dining room and ballroom, would developed a reputation for its fine dining and was a favorite place to dine on special occasions.

The Crystal Room gained national fame by being named "one of America's finest restaurants" in the 1935 book *Adventures in Good Eating* by Duncan Hines (who was already a household name from his brand of food products found in every grocery store). Perhaps the Crystal Room's secret was having a kitchen run and operated exclusively by women. According to Captain H. Mowrey in *Columbus Unforgettables*, Griffith came to the hotel in early 1933 with a mission to polish the silver and bring the hotel back into the prestigious company of his downtown competitors. He surprised many in Columbus when he hired an all-female kitchen crew, including a dietitian, for the hotel. The hotel was the only one in Columbus to have a dietitian on staff, and "she supervised the preservation and the preparation of food for the hotel's customers."

Griffith bragged to his competitors that the change "paid off in more customers because the quality of food was improved." The hotel never had a head chef, and the kitchen was always run like a democracy—from the recipes to the selection of the menu.

Griff, as he was known, set the familial tone of the hotel staff, but he also did some outrageous stunts to attract customers. He once brought a champion steer from the state fair into the lobby, riding the steer all day and proclaiming the hotel had the freshest steaks in the city. This started the Fort Hayes's reputation for great steak dinners.

Mowrey wrote that Griffith left his mark on the hotel during his tenure.

> He always prowled about the hotel looking for things that needed repair or replacement…rebuilt the 14th floor of the hotel into a dozen or more plush bedrooms…On another floor, once a beauty shop, he created a suite, bath in each, of two bedrooms, a built-in bar and a spacious living room facing W. Spring Street. He rated it at $75 a day. It served two couples frequently for birthday or anniversary parties.

The Fort Hayes Crystal Room was a popular place for events and romantic anniversaries. *Columbus Metropolitan Library Image Collection.*

When Griffith retired in 1955, his successor in the manager's office was Thomas S. Walker, a man who regarded himself as a military general and required a military formation for inspection of all the bellboys every morning. After a troop inspection, he would declare, "Dismissed," and the bellboys would march out to begin their days. Mowrey wrote that he was "a most cordial gentleman and when a guest or friend approached, his greeting with a broad smile was, 'Bless you for coming.'"

On February 22, 1968, columnist Johnny Jones wrote a glowing restaurant review on the famous Crystal Room in the *Columbus Dispatch*: "I had dinner there the other evening with friend. It was a joy. The room itself is fascinating. It has suggestions of the period of the 1890s and the 1920s; a flashback to the days when the main dining room of a hotel was the last word in elegance."

The dining room's high ceilings and walls of red velvet–like tapestry (one of the first to be supplied by the Coated Fabrics) created the gay 1890s wall pattern. The chandelier was imported from Czechoslovakia and cost $10,000. Two paintings attracted attention from guests, each by a female French artist. They were originally purchased for the Congress Hotel in Chicago.

The hotel was also known as the Pick-Fort Hayes. In the late 1930s, the Albert Pick Company had thirteen hotels in five states, two of which were in Columbus: the Chittenden Hotel and the Fort Hayes. Other Ohio hotels were the Hotel Miami in Dayton, the Fort Meigs Hotel in Toledo and the Fountain Square Hotel in Cincinnati.

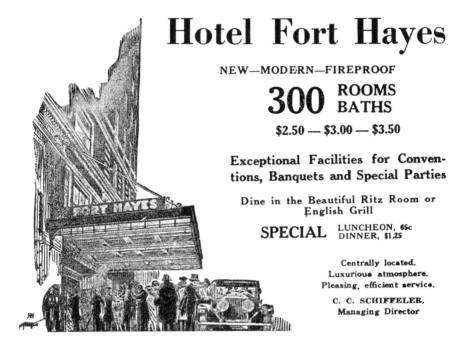

Hotel Fort Hayes

NEW—MODERN—FIREPROOF

300 ROOMS BATHS

$2.50 — $3.00 — $3.50

Exceptional Facilities for Conventions, Banquets and Special Parties

Dine in the Beautiful Ritz Room or English Grill

SPECIAL LUNCHEON, 65c
DINNER, $1.25

Centrally located.
Luxurious atmosphere.
Pleasing, efficient service.

C. C. SCHIFFELER,
Managing Director

An early advertisement of Fort Hayes Hotel. Note the hotel is still advertised as fireproof, underscoring that fires were still on the mind of the public. *Private Collection.*

While the third-largest hotel chain in America seemed stable, the Pick hotels were out of business by the 1970s. It was speculated that they owned too many aging hotels in need of restoration, and consumer taste was favoring a shift to motels outside of city centers. It was the same problem that Columbus's downtown hotels were facing. The Pick Hotels, however, were the first hotels to create a motel chain on a large scale, though they could not compete with other emerging hotel chains. Pick Hotels disappeared after one hundred years in the business.

Like the Seneca, the Fort Hayes Hotel had a number of potential buyers while downtown was changing. Nationwide Insurance, with its national headquarters in Columbus, purchased the Fort Hayes for $2 million in 1973 but declared the hotel a financial liability.

Everyone knew the hotel would be closing. The last hotel manager, Andrew Ginnan, told the *Columbus Dispatch* that, regretfully, the hotel had been "running in the red" for some time and that the new owner "would have to spend a lot of money to make the hotel competitive." He further admitted that the hotel had fallen into disrepair and that seventy-eight rooms had been closed off the year before because they lacked proper furnishings.

Due to rising heating costs, portions of the hotel were sealed off to save money. Ginnan said Nationwide contacted him after the purchase to make preparations for the hotel's closing. At the time, there were twenty-one permanent residents at the hotel whom Nationwide offered to help find housing elsewhere.

The Fort Hayes hung on and remained open for another four years, but everyone knew the hotel was on borrowed time. During the final months of 1976, anticipating the inevitable closing, the Crystal Room was packed almost every evening with patrons remembering old times and cherishing the special restaurant. A massive liquidation sale began—linens, brass handles, china, hangers, TVs and ashtrays. The Great Southern Hotel bought the famous chandelier.

In May 1977, the Fort Hayes closed its doors. Eighty-six employees were left without jobs. The building, a shell, was gutted and demolished.

Katie Griffith, wife of longtime manager Robert Griffith, lived in the hotel from the early 1930s to the late 1950s. When interviewed, she remarked, "I looked at that picture in *The Dispatch* the other night," she said, "and thought, 'there was our dining room behind the windows.' 'There were our bedrooms.' 'Right around the corner there was Bob's room.' That was a hard moment." In recalling how her husband had worked to restore the hotel in the 1930s, she said, "First, all new mattresses, because Griff said the first thing traveling men want is a comfortable bed. Then the kitchen, then the carpets."

Today, the Courtyard Marriott is located near the site of the Fort Hayes Hotel that was, for years, a Central Ohio Transit Authority (COTA) bus depot. Recently, a new downtown COTA bus terminal was built on the site.

THE CHRISTOPHER INN

Dubbed "Roundhouse for the Automobile Age," the Christopher Inn was built in 1963 on the site of the historic Alfred Kelley mansion, built in 1838. This mansion served as the governor's residence from 1890 to 1892. The Greek Revival–style mansion was the home of lawyer, bank, legislator, visionary and canal commissioner Alfred Kelley, who once put his house on the New York Stock Exchange in exchange for bonds to build the canal. For years, schoolchildren knew of it as "the house that saved Ohio." As a very early Greek Revival–style building, it was unusual to find in a city in the wilderness. The Statehouse had not yet been built.

In the last decade of its life, the mansion was the Catholic St. Joseph Cathedral School and owned by the Catholic Diocese of Columbus. Though seemingly safe and eminently conservable, its location on East Broad near Grant Avenue made it vulnerable to future development. Despite the efforts of preservationist Dixey Sayre Miller to find funding or a site for the large building, it was torn down. Hopes were that the building might be reconstructed, and stones were saved at Wolfe Park, though some were lost to flood control in Alum Creek. The majority was sent to the Hale Farm in northern Ohio to be assembled at a later time if more money became available. After five decades of waiting, Miller realized it would not happen in her lifetime and gave her permission that the stones be disposed of if Hale Farm wanted to do so. By then, all the stones had lost their numbers.

Perhaps ironically, the name of the hotel that replaced the Kelley Mansion choose a name evocative of the patron saint of travelers. The Christopher Inn was located at 300 East Broad, next to the Franklin County Memorial Hall (the first Center of Science and Industry, COSI). The memorable circular motor inn had a unique design, and all the rooms on its sixteen floors had curves that required custom furniture with rounded corners in order to fit properly.

There was a circular heated swimming pool, 140 round rooms, Henry's (the stylish modern restaurant) and nightly entertainment. Jack Willey of the *Columbus Dispatch* called the design something out of the future; "towering above E. Broad Street like a rocket ship atop the concrete launching pad that was its parking garage, the Christopher Inn was trumpeted as a contemporary classic."

A prominent example of Mid-century Modern architecture, the Christopher Inn was designed by Leon Ransom. Ransom was the first known African American architect of prominence in Columbus. He worked on major projects, including public libraries and congregate housing. Ransom was born in Columbus on April 29, 1929. Studying at the Catholic University of America, Ransom received a bachelor's degree in geography in 1950 and a master's degree in architecture in 1953. Ransom worked as a registered architect at (Louis) Karlsberger and Associates, beginning in 1954. In 1963, Ransom formed a partnership with Sylvester C. Angel, another black architect in Columbus, to create the firm of Angel and Ransom.

In 1966, Ransom started a solo practice, Leon A. Ransom & Associates, Architects-Planners-Designers. Unfortunately, due to failing health, he gave up the practice in 1970. Following a long illness, Leon Ransom died at the

The Christopher Inn was a unique addition to the Columbus skyline. The architect was African American Leon Ransom. It opened on July 29, 1963. *Private Collection.*

Henry's at the Christopher Inn was decorated in the modern style with white pedestal tables and chairs. The plain walnut paneling gave the feeling of simplicity. *Columbus Metropolitan Library Image Collection.*

young age of forty-two in 1971, and his most famous building in Columbus, the Christopher Inn, is gone.

The Christopher Inn displayed all of the elements of mid-century architecture—simplicity of style, ample windows and open interior spaces. A total of 710 glass panels were used on the exterior. The mezzanine overlooked a thirty-six-foot circular pool and a landscaped stone terrace just outside the pool. A story in the July 24, 1963 *Columbus Citizen-Journal* reported that guests in the hotel's restaurant saw an impressive Broad Street panorama, thanks to the wide sweep of the hotel's trademark glass panels. Rough stone walls were used throughout the hotel's lower levels, along with free-hanging staircases with gold and red carpets throughout.

The Christopher Inn had a short lifespan. Demolition began on June 4, 1988. When the hotel was in the process of being dismantled, the exterior walls came down first, and it now appeared in its partial demolition stage to be the residence of the futuristic cartoon character George Jetson, who could have flown right into his sky-high home.

Fortunately, other examples of Ransom's distinctive style still exist in the Ohio State University Hospital East tower, Columbus Fire Station Eight, the St. Paul AME Annex and the Martin Luther King Jr. Branch public library.

5

AND THEN THERE WAS ONE...WHAT HAPPENED TO THE REST OF THEM?

People noticed when the big hotels went down. Not only were they physical architectural landmarks of a certain size and defining character, but for the average Columbus resident, who never spent nights in a local hotel, the grand Columbus hotels were visited only for celebrations. They were for special occasions like weddings, anniversary dinners and retirement parties (even the longest-employed grave digger at Green Lawn Cemetery in the 1950s was given a surprise retirement dinner at the Deshler). The loss of these hotels left a void in the landscape of the street—sometimes for years—and affected hundreds of people who were left jobless in professions that had little security.

Citizen-Journal columnist Ben Hayes recounted in 1970 that, at one time, the Vendome and the Metropole, both attractive buildings, faced each other across Capital Square. The Hotel Vendome (60 South Third Street) was the fashionable hotel for celebrities, though it had not been built as a hotel. It opened in 1911, renovated and expanded from a former mansion belonging to John Noble of National Hotel fame. It was a five-story, 150-room hotel originally built from the 1898 house. The state had considered buying the mansion, but the hotel had already opened. In 1918, it was purchased by the Young Women's Christian Association as a residence for single young women working in the city and lasted until 1929, when the association constructed a new building on North Fourth Street. The building was demolished in 1932, and a twenty-four-hour Ohio Oil Company service station and parking lot replaced it.

An 1898 photo of the Davidson Hotel on High Street at Naghten operated from 1878 to 1916. It then became the Waldo Hotel. *Columbus Metropolitan Library Image Collection.*

With the loss of the Deshler, the Chittenden, the Fort Hayes and the Virginia, it seemed as though Columbus might be left with only two grand old hotels—the Neil House and the Southern. The Southern had already had a few near-death experiences, and sadly, no one seemed to remember the grandeur of the Hartman because it had not been a hotel for a very long time. It didn't seem to count.

The Hotel Broad Lincoln opened on October 1, 1903, and became the Broad-Lincoln in 1928. It closed in March 1979, the same month it was demolished. *Columbus Metropolitan Library Image Collection.*

With the loss of the Fort Hayes, *Columbus Monthly* writer James Scarff noted that the old hotels that supplied elegance had been undercut by the cheaper, faceless motels and chains that were appearing on the "hyper developed freeway strips." Elegance came with a cost, and no one wanted to pay for it anymore. That was a valid observation. Scarff recounted the growing list of vanishing hotels, but he also offered names of the others that replaced them. The Christopher Inn replaced the Broad-Lincoln, the Sheraton replaced the Virginia and Lazarus Department Store replaced the United States Hotel.

The Bliss Hotel (606–16 South High) in 1926 was leased to E.D. Sullivan, described as a veteran hotel man, for $250,000 and ninety-nine years, making it the largest real estate deal ever done on South High Street after the Southern Hotel. Sullivan had been associated with the Norwich, the Deshler, the Hartman, the Columbus and the Rol-Eddy.

The Bliss was a four-story, fireproof concrete building erected in 1924. It was said to be the only hotel in the city with all steel furniture, and the hotel felt it had attractions that could compete with the older hotels. There was an auto dealer on the ground level. The thirty-four rooms had circulating ice water, built-in bathtubs, a restaurant and the latest in heating. Thirty rooms did not have baths. With the exception of the marble staircase, there appeared to be an emphasis on functionality over luxury. However, the front doors were said to cost $5,000.00. Sullivan had plans to sell part of the hotel to permanent guests and charge rates of $1.50 to $2.00 for others. The Bliss lasted for many years, but its future was tied to a location that could not successfully weather the times—closure of the breweries, the Great Depression, loss of nearby commercial activity, lack of city investment in post–World War II and eventually the plans for freeways.

A good location, however, did not guarantee prosperity. In the 1980s, the manager of the Neil House was adamant that the Neil House was not going to be torn down—it actually had parking. Everyone seemed quick to blame the loss of hotels (and other buildings in the downtown) on the post–World War II frenzy for a faster-paced life, the surge of cars and the need for parking lots. But hotels were being torn down or repurposed for a very long time and for a variety of reasons.

The history of hotels in Columbus is the history of constant movement, changing names and reinventing businesses from stagecoach days through World War I. The Columbus Inn was torn down in 1854. One of two hotels called the National Hotel disappeared (as did others clustered around the Union Depot) with the building of the viaducts over the railroad tracks.

In 1903, the *Columbus Evening Dispatch* featured the exciting growth of the city with a look back at Columbus through the city directories of the 1840s through the 1870s. Of particular note were the hotels that had been listed in 1843. Most were gone even though they were less than fifty years old. While there was a nod to nostalgia, there also seemed to be a sense of validity that this was a sign of "a remarkable progress—[one] that gave movement in all lines of business activity." The progress would push Columbus into the front rank of the great cities of the "middle west." The railways were to be the great arteries that would carry the "rich blood of the city into distant parts of the state, with every throb of the great heart, awakening to new life the villages and countryside through which they pass."

Unfortunately, no one would have been able to predict in 1903 that in fifty years, the railroads would have a coronary, and the hotels would be among the first victims. The new twentieth-century Columbus was passive aggressive about progress. The old was mourned, but the new meant more life blood. And as long as there was a Neil House, a Deshler and a Southern (and, it seemed in most minds, there always would be), it was acceptable for the old to make room for the new.

The old pioneer establishments, especially if they were frame construction, and the smaller hotels faded away all the time—the City House, Smith's European Hotel, the Wattshier, the Union, the Tenny, the Utopia, the McMordie, the Newel, Hotel Victoria, the Spencer House, the Stag and others. Most left without even a mention in the newspaper, though to be fair, some had been boardinghouses that used the name "hotel" while others had ceased being hotels and were, by the time of their demises, anonymous commercial buildings.

Even the substantial and truly beautiful buildings that faced the Statehouse—the Metropole and the Vendome—left relatively quietly and are remembered mostly by antique dealers who bought the marble mantels. The Metropole, at 71 South High Street, was five stories tall and had Italianate architecture with heavily hooded widows, massive brackets along

The Vendome Hotel was formerly the private home of John Noble (associated with the National Hotel) and operated from 1898 to 1919. It was taken over by the YWCA and was demolished in June 1932. *Columbus Metropolitan Library Image Collection.*

a line of frieze windows and a pediment almost a story tall. By World War I, it had been demolished to make room for the Majestic Theater, which, in turn, gave way to the Green Department Store.

In 1914, the old Irving Hotel on East Broad Street, later called Trinity House (owned by Dr. Samuel B. Hartman), was razed for the new Athletic Club. Irving Hotel/Trinity House had been a former girls' school turned temporary hospital in the Civil War and was later repurposed as a boardinghouse/hotel, operated by Mrs. Linville and her mother for more than twenty years.

The former Kaiserhof Hotel and Garden on West Gay Street closed due to bankruptcy in January 1919. A small, three-story building just south of Wall Alley, it sadly suffered from a decline in business during World War I (possibly due to its unfortunate name). Over $2,000 was due to three creditors—$1,400 to a cigar company. The property was owned by the Hoster-Columbus Associated Breweries, which was facing the prospects of Prohibition. Unlike the Irving House, the Kaiserhof Hotel building still stands. Easily noticed on West Gay Street for its distinctive "Dutch" roof, the building's past as a hotel is forgotten. A few probably remember it from the 1960s as the home of Larry Flynt's *Hustler* magazine enterprise (with an illegal topless bar in the basement).

The Star Hotel (on North High Street near Union Station) survived a devastating fire in 1923. It was leased to Sullivan (who later acquired the Bliss Hotel), and Laura Hanna and Frank Powell (also associated with Columbus hotels) pledged to reopen the hotel after it was reconstructed, adding hot and cold water to each of the 150 rooms. They hoped to put it on par with the two other hotels—the Norwich and the Columbus—that were also owned by Sullivan. The building was eventually demolished.

In the court of popular opinion, there were signs that too much was happening too quickly and behind closed doors. The popular columnists of the Columbus papers from the 1960s through the 1990s—Johnny Jones (*Columbus Dispatch*), Ben Hayes (*Citizen-Journal*), Jack Wiley (*Citizen-Journal*) and Mike Harden (*Columbus Dispatch*)—were often the closest to the ins and outs of the hotel business. Because they covered many of the human interest stories in those years, they relied on personal relationships with the management of the hotels, and because the hotel business had always been an intimate fraternity of innkeepers, they knew each other's business and felt each other's pain. There were probably no greater storytellers or observers of human nature than those who worked in hotels, so the demise of not just the grande dames but also the smaller hotels was like a death blow to those columnists.

In 1968, Johnny Jones met with personal friends William Dunn and Charles Duffy of the Neil House and Tom Sabrey of the Deshler-Beasley. (Dunn also worked at the Virginia.) Together, the four men reminisced—about R.I. Griffith, who had paid top money for the best cattle at the Ohio State Fair and then brought them into the lobby of the Fort Hayes; the differences between the Deshler-Wallick and the Deshler-Beasley management styles; the deals between the Seneca and the Southern; the whispering booths of the Neil where politicians and lobbyists huddled; the swanky opening night of the expansion of the Deshler with the mayor of New York; and the "hot spots" for the old-timers at the Jefferson, the Columbus, the Bliss, the Farmers' Hotel and the Normandie. They spoke like old men on borrowed time. Jones already had written about the impending loss of the old State Hotel at 34 West State Street. He felt that if buildings in downtown kept coming down for parking lots, very soon only the AIU (LeVeque Tower) and "a lot of parking lots" would remain, and that was in 1942. Little time was left when they met in 1968. In 1969, the Deshler Hotel was torn down.

Some hotels, like the State Hotel, fell victim to urban renewal before the term was even conceived. West State and Front Streets was the center of nightlife in Columbus in the 1920s and 1930s—the naughty side to the back of the Neil House. The State Hotel was part of the little red-light district (ironically, now the Judicial Center) where many of the theater people stayed. When Al G. Fields had his minstrel show in town, the troupe wintered at the State Hotel. The rates were reasonable, and during Prohibition, there was always booze to be had in a centralized secret spot in the alley. Really good half pints were hidden in the hedges of the lawn of the Statehouse.

Hotel guests could enjoy Bobby Burn's saloon or Jack Weber's nude back bar or the good food at Mose Topoloosky's, all of which were the State Hotel's neighbors. When the State Hotel came down, the regular patrons moved to Corrodi's on West State and then to the Knickenbocker (before it became a burlesque house) on South High Street. The Knickenbocker was lost to the building of City Center; City Center was just lost. Today, new downtown living (as there would have been in Columbus from the 1820s through the 1950s) emerges on the site of the Commons.

The loss of others reflected national changes in transportation. Columbus had once been known as a "crossroads city" that grew from stages to canals, National Road to railroads. Now it seemed to be a fly-over city, even though Columbus's Port Columbus terminal marked the beginning of transcontinental air flight (which was also tied to rail connections, unfortunately).

Views of the parlor, office and guest and dining rooms in the Bryden Hotel at 177 East Town Street. The Bryden operated from 1900 to 1922 and then became the Clayton Hotel in 1923. *Columbus Metropolitan Library Image Collection.*

In 1931, fifty-four hotels in less than a two-mile radius of the Statehouse were listed in the city directory. Most of the smaller hotels are completely unknown today—the Athens, the Bartoes, the Broad, the Capital, the Central, the Coranado, the Edsell, the Farmers, the Foremans, two Franklin Hotels, the Gay-Manor, the Gem, the Goodale, Hotel Columbus, Hotel Domicile, Hotel Elwood, Hotel Fairfax, Hotel Jefferson, Hotel Manhattan, Hotel Oak, Hotel Pal, Hotel Rector, Hotel Sattler, Hotel William, Hotel Winston, the Lennox Hotel, the Litchferd Hotel, the New Bryden Hotel, the Ohio, the Palace, the Park, the Plaza, the Roe-Eddy, the Shively, the Star, the State, the Vincent, the Waldo and the Willard.

By contrast, in 1956, *Columbus: This Week* (a weekly pamphlet on downtown events and places of interest) had already downsized itself to a metropolitan pamphlet that served Columbus, Springfield and Dayton. Contradictions (in hindsight) are apparent. Because the small publication was now a monthly, it had less space for advertising from Columbus businesses. A full page read: "Columbus' Rapid Growth for…BOOMTOWN, U.S.A…Ohio's Capital is in Period of Unprecedented Growth." Except, there was no boom. While promoting annual rainfall, low population of foreign-born citizens and miles of sewers, the number of daily passenger trains through Union Station was sixty-six, served by two railroads—perhaps a third of what had come

J.T. Gratigny was the proprietor of the Star Hotel. It was later known as the Rol-Eddy Hotel and the Reid Hotel. It was destroyed by fire in February 1923. *Columbus Metropolitan Library Image Collection.*

through Columbus and originally necessitated the hotel building boom. Only fourteen hotels advertised.

As the number of hotels suffered economic hard times, the number of rooms available for conventions also fell off. The spiral downward was partly

An early photo of the Star Hotel. *Library of Congress.*

self-fulfilling prophecy and partly the inability, despite good efforts, to stop the now bleeding heart of the hotel business.

The Hotel Jefferson, at 17 East Spring Street, opened on May 25, 1907, in a building first constructed in 1890 by Edward Mithoff, whose family had come to Columbus in the 1850s. The original building was named the Hanover Block, for Mithoff's birthplace in Germany, and it opened as apartments for permanent residents. The six-story handsome, dark brick apartments became a hotel with seventy-three modern rooms that hoped to capture the city's convention trade with low rates of two to six dollars a week. It was renamed to honor Thomas Jefferson. Sixty-eight years later almost to the day of its opening, plans were announced to sell the contents of the hotel, as it would close on May 15, 1977. Nicholas Mithoff, Edward's great-grandson, owned the hotel. The furniture, desks, doors and other contents were expected to bring $25,000. While there were no immediate plans for the building, the offices on the ground floor and the tavern would remain open. Tenants were being removed to live at the Norwich Hotel nearby. In 1975, it was announced that within six months, the Hotel Jefferson would be torn down. Today, it is a parking lot for a copy store.

The Columbus Hotel at 235–43 East Long was built in 1912 and was described as "a popular hostelry" on the European plan with a restaurant. The location, several blocks from the Statehouse, had been chosen specifically to serve the convention trade as it was very close to Memorial Hall on East Broad Street. The six-story hotel was most notable architecturally for its heavy projecting cornices supported by massive brackets.

It was owned for a time in the early 1920s by E.D. Sullivan, who had acquired the Star and the Norwich Hotels. When it was leased to the Central Ohio Land Company in 1929, it was described as a fireproof structure containing 190 guest rooms, a ballroom, a dining room, a lobby and a number of storerooms. In its final days sixty years later, the once-beautiful Columbus Hotel was described as having 100 rooms, a failed heating system and a failing metal cornice. It also suffered from tangled ownership by two different entities and a ninety-nine-year lease from 1929. Only the cost of razing such a large building (which the city would have to pay) kept the building standing.

On January 31, 1977, the tenants, many senior citizens with no family near, were taken to Krumm Recreation Center by the Red Cross, the Columbus Police and the Ohio National Guard. On January 30, the city had closed

A bellman (far left) stands ready to assist the next guest in the lobby of the Hotel Columbus on Long Street, circa 1912. *Columbus Metropolitan Library Image Collection.*

A 1979 photo showing the Columbus Hotel located at the corner of East Long and Fifth Streets. *Grandview Heights Public Library.*

the hotel when the temperature inside fell below freezing. Most expected and welcomed the move, a temporary one until other arrangements could be made, because they were now warm and had access to showers and hot water. One senior joked that the move was interrupting his love life.

Guests converse in front of the cigar stand in the Hotel Columbus, circa 1912. The hotel would mature in its final years as a dwelling for seniors on fixed incomes. *Columbus Metropolitan Library Image Collection.*

In 1979, the Columbus City Council voted to reverse its earlier decision to allow the Columbus Hotel to remain for 128 days. The city code enforcement officer asked the city council members to authorize the building's demolition "before somebody gets killed." The opposing side had hoped a foreclosure and a sheriff's sale would clear the title to the building and a new owner would rehabilitate the hotel. But there were already dozens of liens against the building, and it seemed doubtful that someone would invest in even a reduced appraised price. The Columbus Hotel was razed at the city's expense.

The fate of the Charminel (324 East State Street) was much more prolonged. The Charminel was a twelve-story hotel completed in March 1925 and owned by Dr. Charles Bowen, a prominent X-ray specialist and colleague of the founder of Grant Hospital, Dr. James Baldwin. The hotel was built to accommodate the overnight patients for Grant Hospital across the street. The hotel's unusual name came from a combination of family names, Char (for Charles Bowen), Min (for Minne Bowen, his wife) and El (for Elizabeth Bowen, his daughter).

The Charminel Hotel had forty four-room apartments, completely furnished down to silverware and dishes and offered maid service. There was a restaurant but also kitchens for the suites. There was a living room and a

The Hotel Columbus opened on July 7, 1912, and remained in business for the next sixty-five years, closing in early 1977. *Columbus Metropolitan Library Image Collection.*

dressing room with a bed that folded into the wall. There were private phones for each room and a switchboard for long-distance calls. The upper floors had two front apartments, one of which was occupied by the Bowen family.

The hotel did very well and, in later years, was considered to be like the Normandie, "an acceptable address for Columbus residents," according to Bob Thomas in his book *Columbus Unforgettables*. It was acquired by Harry Gilbert, a well-known Columbus shoe retailer, who "kept it up in a most presentable way." It passed among other owners for years.

Downtown florist Lou Viereck purchased the building in the 1970s and claimed "the penthouse," once occupied by the Bowens, as his own "crow's nest." He operated it as a residential hotel. Though Viereck had running feuds with the city over issues like shoveling the snow from sidewalks in front of his shop on East State, his greatest battle was yet to come in the 1990s and would be played out many times in the newspapers in 1991.

Ever a frugal man, Viereck's battles with the city usually involved the cost of snow removal but now it was over numerous code violations at the hotel—exposed wires, leaky pipes and rodent infestation. The city filed a $1.2 million suit against Viereck to force the installation of a fire alarm system. Many of the eighty-plus tenants, Viereck countered, were there because they had no money, so how was he, the owner, responsible for it, and where would they go if the city gave evictions orders. Tenants, for the most part, sided with Viereck.

The eighty-seven-year-old Viereck hustled to comply, and the court agreed he had held up his part of the bargain (the fire alarm and smoker detector systems were on their ways to being finished). One month later, the city put him on notice that he and the tenants would be evicted in two weeks because not enough had been completed. The next month, Viereck received another extension from the courts. By December 1991, Viereck had been fined $71,000 for failure to repair the Charminel. Tenants began to move out, and city council voted $10,000 to help relocate them.

In January 1992, city and county officers armed with shotguns (who feared armed disgruntled tenants inside), city and county officials (who wanted to be sure justice was done), the remainder of the tenants (who huddled in the January cold with their meager belongings), abandoned animals (that were headed for the humane society), two non-tenants (who included a homeless fifteen-year-old girl) and dozens of reporters (who wanted to be eye-witnesses to the final story) swarmed the area. The Charminel was closed. The fire that all feared did not happen, and the building sat abandoned for four more years. Grant Medical Center purchased the Charminel in 1995, and the building was torn down.

The Normandie Hotel was one of the many hotels on East Long Street that, like the Columbus Hotel hoped to take advantage of convention trade. Built in the 1890s when that part of Long Street was still cow pastures, the Normandie was managed by Foster Burdell. Burdell also managed the Seneca Hotel. He knew the area had been a cow pasture because two Jersey cows were still permanent lodgers of the space.

The success of the Normandie was, in part, responsible for the development of an active business association that viewed High Street as a river of commerce and felt Long Street could be one of its major tributaries.

The Normandie catered to families and supplied apartments with a home-like atmosphere. The Columbus Hotel, on the other hand, was strictly for commercial travelers who wanted a modern hotel and a place to meet with business associates for lunch or dinner. Though these two hotels were promoted as important factors in the growth of the area, concerned Long Street businessmen had another reason to see them as investments: they were owned by white businessmen.

Long Street from High Street eastward was poised for change in the first decade of the twentieth century, with the construction of the new Capital Trust building (now the Atlas building). Designed by Frank Packard, a prominent Columbus architect, the new building also housed a private club, the Ohio Club, on its upper floors. This building replaced a corner of an old African American business district in the area once called the Badlands. The Badlands had developed between Union Depot and downtown and was considered highly undesirable by city fathers. As it grew east and south, Long Street was considered the new line that should not be crossed. Black churches and businessmen pushed back, with St. Paul's AME Church making its stand at Jefferson Avenue and East Long Street.

In time, the Normandie was torn down. Today, the Normandy is opening as exclusive apartments, a northward expansion of the new urban living on Gay Street, and reclaiming the old Welsh Church on East Long as a fitness/spa center for the new residents.

The St. Clair is a hotel that was not built to be a hotel and—though it remains—also figured into the color lines that segregated Columbus. The St. Clair (338–46 St. Clair Avenue) started life as a private hospital in 1911, opened by a group of doctors to serve that part of the city. The operating room was located on the top floor with skylights for northern exposure, which was customary. In 1916, it was used, perhaps primarily, as a hospital for railroad workers from the Pennsylvania Railroad. The four-story building was a major part of a larger complex that included the house next door, which was used as a nurses' training center.

As the neighborhood changed, private hospitals—which were often small facilities—did not survive. The St. Clair hospital became a convalescent home operated by the Garrett family. In 1948, the family converted it into a hotel that filled the need for comfortable and affordable accommodations for African Americans who were discriminated against when trying to find lodgings downtown.

William and Zylphia Garrett, who operated it from 1948 to 1976, made the hotel extremely popular, which was complemented by its location near Mt. Vernon Avenue and East Long Street. The Near East Side was famous for its jazz clubs and theaters that featured local and national black performers. While headliners might be invited to play at the Neil or Deshler Hotels, black performers were not welcomed guests, and the St. Clair provided accommodations, as well as a location near the after-hours clubs. Duke Ellington and his band, Count Basie and his band and Lionel Hampton stayed at the St. Clair.

Boardinghouses and commercial buildings on the Near East Side often were used as hotels for African American guests. Many are not well documented; others, like the Macon Hotel, have sketchy records. The Macon Hotel (residential rooms above retail space) is documented in city directories from the late 1930s to the early 1940s.

In 2002, the St. Clair was reborn and dedicated as the St. Clair Senior Apartments through an extensive collaborate partnership that involved the city, the Christian Community Development Corporation, banks and state institutions and Fred Schwab, a Grandview architect. The building is on the National Register of Historic Places.

In 1986, the Norwich Hotel was part of a new plan to repurpose downtown buildings, including former hotels. The Joseph Skilken Company and the architects in charge—Cline, Daniel and Associates—recognized the building's Art Nouveau style was worth investing in. Like other aging hotels, the Norwich had elderly tenants who needed to be relocated. The Joseph Skilken Company donated the beds, dressers, night stands and chairs to tenants who wanted or needed them and helped them find new homes. Lyda Spencer, age 101, who described herself as a "career girl," having lived in the downtown area since 1933 and worked as a Statehouse secretary for thirty-nine years, was one of the last to go.

The Norwich Hotel (and Annex) at the northwest corner of East State and North Fourth Streets was built about 1890. Its architect was Elah Terrell, who also designed the old Board of Trade building and the Broad Street Presbyterian Church. It was designed for Henry Lanman, an important person at the Board of Trade and at the Broad Street Presbyterian Church. As a corner building, the hotel's Romanesque Revival style, with terra cotta ornamentation and corner turrets added interesting lines to an otherwise modest six-story building. It also has made the building recognizable, though probably most who pass it do not know much about its history.

Noverre Musson, a distinguished Columbus architect and frequent architectural commentator, saw the saving of the Norwich Hotel as

A view looking northeast at the Norwich Hotel on the corner of East State Street and South Forth Street. The building was constructed around 1890 and was remodeled into offices and retail space in 1985. *Columbus Metropolitan Library Image Collection.*

significant as the restoration of the Old Post Office (Bricker and Eckler), Katherine LeVeque's work at the Palace Theater and Ron Pizzuti's purchase of the old Copco warehouse (North Fifth between Spring and Naghten Streets). In short, he saw the corner turning in downtown when "the entrepreneurs in

An early advertisement for the Hotel Norwich, which might not originally have been built to be a hotel. *Columbus Metropolitan Library Image Collection.*

our midst, who in the past would have torn down fine buildings and replaced them with new, have been encouraged to reexamine the existing buildings. Restoration and reuse have become stylish and profitable."

The original double-huge windows (sadly, now gone) suggested that the building might have started life as a commercial structure since the size of the windows would have been unusual in a hotel. The annex, which became part of the hotel in 1921, was probably built for commercial and department stores. The building has been altered a number of times—the first time in 1935.

The last hotel associated with the downtown hotels, the trains and the early commerce of the late nineteenth and early twentieth centuries also went—not with a whimper but with a bang. In 1991, the fight to save the Northern Hotel in the North Market district (now the Short North District) was a classic divide between developers and historic preservationists, with the city on both sides over whether an original High Street hotel building would remain standing or be torn down to make way for planned renovations for the emerging district.

The Northern Hotel—a round-turreted, four-story brick building at 491–501 North High Street—was on the site of the former Park Hotel, and many of its architectural features and the profile of the building were reasons to believe that it was built from parts of the Park Hotel. In May 1990, the Columbus Development Commission upended a condemnation order on the vacant Northern Hotel. The owner of the building was given thirty days to develop a renovation plan.

The North Market Commission and the North Market Development Authority were concerned about the loss of two buildings (the Northern and an adjacent building) and the future of the North Market, which was under study. The market was to move out of the Quonset hut and into a former warehouse on Front Street (where it currently is). Another stakeholder in the area envisioned a multistory parking lot on the site of the Quonset hut once the North Market moved into the Front Street warehouse. Others contended that the proposed parking lot would doom the character of the market district.

Because the building of the Convention Center had been delayed, a great deal of uncertainty hung over what the right option was. The Ohio Historic Preservation Office also warned that the loss of buildings could jeopardize the integrity of the National Register district. The Division of Regulations of the City, on the other hand, ordered emergency demolitions in April 1991 based on the liability of the city in the case of fire or structural collapse. Preservation groups—Citizens for a Better Skyline and Columbus Landmarks Foundation—countered the logic. The previous year's inspection showed the building was sound. The North Market Commission also said the issue was one of demolition by neglect on the part of the owner.

The North Market Commission and the Division of Regulations were both city agencies. On April 23, 1991, the Columbus Building Commission, after hearing all sides, voted 4–0 to uphold the city's request for an emergency demolition order. On April 24, the Loewendick Company began demolition, but the arguments were about more than one old hotel. Chris Steele, president of Citizens for a Better Skyline, questioned the city's commitment to historic structures. Michael Shannon, regulations administrator for the city, said, "This was no doubt an issue of historic preservation versus public safety and outweighed historic preservation." Pat Schmucki of *Columbus Live* had another viewpoint—"What a way to celebrate Earth Day…no recycling or reuse of resources."

However, the issues raised in this final fight for an old hotel (the Northern), the interest generated when the last grande dame was saved (the Southern), the social issues illuminated by the plight of elderly and homeless hotel residents (the Columbus, the Normandie and the Charminel), the pride reflected in reusing a cultural resource that marked a painful period of history (the St. Clair), the insights learned in wise or poor urban planning decisions (the Neil, the Deshler, and the Hartman) and the stories passed down to give insight to Columbus's history (the Virginia, the Seneca, the Park, the American House and others) also mean that hotels did more than provide a place for travelers. Hotels influenced and were influenced by political, historical, economic, social and urban identity issues.

EPILOGUE

Today, on the mezzanine level outside the ballroom, the Great Southern Fireproof Hotel pays tribute to its four grand sister hotels of Columbus (the Deshler, the Neil House, the Hartman and the Chittenden) with paintings and rooms named in honor of them. Sadly, only one other grande dame remains standing today: the Hartman Hotel. These hotels represented a new era of Columbus—an era of wealth, class, extravagant spending and incredible design.

Throughout the writing of this book, something once said by celebrated historian David McCullough came to mind many times, and I thought I would share:

> *History is not about dates and quotes and obscure provisos. History is about life, about change, about consequences, cause and effect. It's about the mystery of human nature, the mystery of time. And it isn't just about politics, the military and social issues, which is almost always the way it's taught…it's about music and poetry and drama and science, and medicine and money and love.*

The historic hotels were not only a luxurious (and sometimes not-so-lovely) place for travelers to rest and spend the night, but hotels were also part of the tangible fabric of our community. They were destinations for families to spend time together over an elegant dinner on a special occasion. They were places to shop and buy a special gift for a grandparent or teacher. They were places for a romantic getaway. They were places to attend concerts and experience the arts. They were important meeting places to discuss political and social issues. They were places for secrets,

A postcard of the grand hotels in 1916 featured the Neil House, the Deshler, the Chittenden, the Hartman and the Great Southern Hotels. *Private Collection.*

As downtown changed in the mid-twentieth century, it seemed as though the landmark third Neil House would be there forever. However, as the streetscape of High Street changed, older hotels were revealed. The nineteenth-century American House Hotel was actually still embedded in the back wall of Kresge Dime Store, seen to the left of the picture. *Private Collection.*

rendezvous and sometimes just to think. They were places to buy a postcard, a newspaper, a cup of coffee or a beer. They were places to hide out or live it up. They were places for blue-collar shirts and Prince Albert coats, French chefs and immigrants, fathers of five and childless widows. They were launch pads for political careers and places of solace for the losers.

Hotels were not only important for guests, visitors and patrons, but they also were the central hub of our cities. They were the epicenter for a different kind of family: the hotel staff, many of whom did not have families of their own and formed lifelong working and personal friendships.

While researching each hotel, we almost always came across stories of people who worked at one particular hotel for most of their lives and were devastated when it closed, but they maintained fond memories of what once had been. In some cases, the hotel business was a family affair: from the owners to the hotel managers to the front desk clerks down to the bellboys and maids. In other cases, hotels were home to governors, politicians, bachelors and older folks on fixed incomes.

John H. Glenn Jr. and his wife, Annie, shown in their hotel room at the Neil House, waiting for early election returns in his race to become U.S. senator on November 5, 1974. *Grandview Heights Public Library.*

The razing of the Deshler Hotel, which happened during the week of April 15, 1970. *Grandview Heights Public Library.*

Hotels seemed to be permanent fixtures in the community until the first-generation hotels passed away. They reflected American history and culture—technology, architecture, values, culture, war, crime, entertainment, foreign affairs, policy and change.

We approached the idea of the hotel as a historic artifact—a window through which to see the people of Columbus in a historical context. Hotels were monuments to the city—a showcase for the architects, engineers, builders, owners, businessmen and developers.

There is sadness that many of the monuments to Columbus are no longer standing, but that sadness also reminds us to cherish the structures that have endured—the grande dame and its more modest sisters.

The stories we uncovered for this book remind us that everyone has a story—the young Dunn siblings growing up in the Virginia Hotel, Mrs. Hartman and her quest for instant hot water, Harry and Bess Truman being stalked by teenage girls, Chittenden's determination that no fire would ever stop him from his dream, the Fort Hayes manager parading a cow in the hotel lobby to sell his steaks and Raul Castro's heated argument at the Seneca front desk over charges. At present, the United States is in the process of reestablishing relations with Cuba. If Rhodebeck is still alive, she would make a feisty American ambassador to Cuba.

TOM BETTI

BIBLIOGRAPHY

Algeo, Matthew. *Harry Truman's Excellent Adventure*. Chicago: Chicago Review Press, 2009.

Arter, Bill. *Columbus Vignettes*. Vols. 1–4. Columbus, OH: Nida-Eckstein Printing Inc., 1966–1971.

Cole, Charles C., Jr. *A Fragile Capital: Identity and the Early Years of Columbus, Ohio*. Columbus: Ohio State University Press, 2001.

Dudgeon, Thomas H. "The Press Club of Ohio." In *More Columbus Unforgettables*, edited by Robert D. Thomas, 159–161. Columbus, OH: Robert D. Thomas, 1986.

Eisenberg, Sidney. "A Neil House Secret." In *Columbus Unforgettables*, Vol. II, edited by Robert Thomas Columbus. N.p., 1963.

Garrett, Betty. *America's Crossroads*. Tulsa, OK: Continental Heritage Press, 1980.

Gerber, David A. *Black Ohio and the Color Line, 1860–1915*. Urbana: University of Illinois Press, 1976.

Gold, David M. *Democracy in Session: A History of the Ohio General Assembly*. Athens: Ohio University Press, 2009.

Hardin, Mike. *Columbus Celebrates the Millennium*. Montgomery, AL: Community Communications Inc., 2000.

Hooper, Osman Castle. *History of City of Columbus*. Columbus, OH: Memorial Publishing Company, 1925.

Howe, Henry. *Historical Collections of Ohio*. 2nd ed. Cincinnati: State of Ohio, 1904.

Industries of Ohio: Columbus, Historical and Descriptive Review, Business and Businessmen in 1878. Columbus, OH: Historical Publishing Company, 1878.

Ireland, W.A., H.J. Westerman and Ray Rohn. *Club Men of Columbus in Caricature*. East Aurora, NY: Roycrofters, 1911.

Lathrop's Columbus Directory. Columbus, OH: Richard Nevins Printer, 1862.

Lee, Alfred. *History of the City of Columbus*. 2 vols. New York: Munsell, 1892.

Lentz, Ed. "American House Hotel—a Piece of the Past is Gone." *This Week*, March 27, 1995.

————. *The Story of a City*. Charleston, SC: Arcadia Publishing, 2003.

Mowery, H. "Front Boy." In *Columbus Unforgettables*, edited by Robert D. Thomas. Columbus, OH: Robert D. Thomas, 1987.

Poivre d'Arvor, Patrick. *First Class: Legendary Train Journeys Around the World*. New York: Vendome Press, 2007.

Samuelson, Robert, Pasquale Grado, Judith Kitchen and Jeffrey Darbee. *Architecture: Columbus*. Columbus, OH: Foundation of the Columbus Chapter of the American Institute of Architects, 1976.

Sandoval-Strausz, A.K. *Hotel: An American History*. New Haven, CT: Yale University Press, 2007.

Scarff, James. "Now There are Two," *Columbus Monthly*, n.d.

Seifert, Myron T. "Columbus Inns, Taverns" and "Columbus Hotels—Grows with the Years in Number and Luxurious Accommodations Provided for Patrons." File, Columbus Metropolitan Library.

INDEX

ABOUT THE AUTHORS

Tom Betti is dedicated to bringing history to life through entertaining storytelling. He co-leads the Historic Tavern Tours with Doreen, bringing dry humor and wit. He served on the board of the Columbus Landmarks Foundation for two full terms and chaired the education committee charged with leading the organization's educational tours and extensive programming. He earned a master's in history from Norwich University. Tom has coauthored several books on local Columbus history with Doreen, available through The History Press. A native of the Cleveland, Ohio area, it is fitting that his condo resides in the historic 1898 Hartman Hotel building in Columbus, Ohio. He lives with his Boston terrier, Hugo.

Doreen Uhas Sauer is a longtime Columbus educator with Columbus City and has worked extensively in international civic education. She served as board president for the Columbus Landmarks Foundation and on a number of boards in the University District, where she is active in historic preservation, urban issues and local history. She has received statewide recognition for her work in preservation education, developed more than thirty local history/architecture programs and was named Ohio Teacher of the Year. She has coauthored several books on local Columbus history and the University District, where she resides with her husband, John, whose roots are extensive in the German South Side.